Fred D'Aguiar was born in London in 1960 and raised in Guyana and south-east London. He now lives in Florida, where he teaches English at the University of Miami. Author of three novels and four books of poetry, he has been awarded the T. S. Eliot Prize for poetry, the Guyanese National Poetry Award and the Malcolm X prize for poetry. He also won the 1994 Whitbread First Novel Award for his novel *The Longest Memory*.

ALSO BY FRED D'AGUIAR

Fiction

The Longest Memory
Dear Future
Feeding the Ghosts

Poetry

Mama Dot
Airy Hall
British Subjects
Bill of Rights

Plays

A Jamaican Airman Foresees His Death

Fred D'Aguiar

BLOODLINES

VINTAGE

Published by Vintage 2001

2 4 6 8 10 9 7 5 3 1

Copyright © Fred D'Aguiar 2000

Fred D'Aguiar has asserted his right under the Copyright,
Designs and Patents Act 1988 to be identified as the author
of this work

First published in Great Britain by
Chatto & Windus 2000

Vintage
Random House, 20 Vauxhall Bridge Road,
London SW1V 2SA

Random House Australia (Pty) Limited
20 Alfred Street, Milsons Point, Sydney
New South Wales 2061, Australia

Random House New Zealand Limited
18 Poland Road, Glenfield,
Auckland 10, New Zealand

Random House (Pty) Limited
Endulini, 5A Jubilee Road, Parktown 2193,
South Africa

The Random House Group Limited Reg. No. 954009
www.randomhouse.co.uk

A CIP catalogue record for this book
is available from the British Library

ISBN 0 09 928442 1

The Random House Group Limited supports The Forest Stewardship
Council (FSC®), the leading international forest certification organisation.
Our books carrying the FSC label are printed on FSC® certified paper.
FSC is the only forest certification scheme endorsed by the leading
environmental organisations, including Greenpeace. Our
paper procurement policy can be found at
www.randomhouse.co.uk/environment

MIX
Paper from
responsible sources

FSC
www.fsc.org   FSC® C018072

Printed and bound in Great Britain by Clays Ltd, St Ives PLC

Contents

Acknowledgements

My thanks to the editors of the following periodicals in which parts of *Bloodlines* have appeared: *Callaloo* (USA), *The Caribbean Writer* (Virgin Islands), *Heat* (Australia), *Landfall* (New Zealand), *Poetry Review* (UK).

Thanks also to Farrar Straus and Giroux for permission to quote the lines from Eugenio Montale's *Cuttlefish Bones* which appear in their edition of Montale's *Collected Poems 1920–1954*, translated by Jonathan Galassi.

I benefited from the advice of a number of people who very kindly agreed to read *Bloodlines*. My gratitude to Geoff Hardy, Grace Theriault, Doug Mayfield, Graeme Rigby and Rebecca Carter, who is a gifted editor, and to Debbie Dalton as always.

For Baba Christopher

This, today, is all that we can tell you:
what we are not, what we do not want.
                    Eugenio Montale

I and I

Word goes I born with a full head of weed
cut by my owner and stones in my mouth
she pulled before she let me take my first feed.
I could see clearly the moment I popped out
how my life would be because I had two seeds
between my legs and a pointer due South.
I should mention that my two seeds brown;
in this time brown did not stick around.

You guessed correct. My earthly father white,
my mother, black. Two trains on one track
thundering towards each other at night,
neither willing nor able to stop and back
the fuck up regardless who more right
than who, each looking through a crack
at the other and seeing only one gesture,
the old, backwards facing two-finger.

Had she hidden from him or he ignored her,
instead of neither giving way that night or day
on those proverbial tracks, I would not be here.
I'd be a figment in your mind, a mandalay
(I looked it up) or wraith, if it's ghosts you prefer
to something substantial handed you on a tray;
not this body with two bloodlines in its veins,
nor this death-in-life caused by those two trains.

As usual, I am running ahead of myself,
too eager to divulge how I cannot die,
can't be killed, buried, put on a shelf
in a crypt, or snuffed out, even if I try,
as I found when my one true love left
me for another and yours truly climbed a sky-
scraper (this is in my modern phase),
jumped and landed splat and got up dazed.

My six-foot-one, two-twenty-pound frame
mixes two skin tones and matches my brown eyes.
My knotted black hair and broad nose came
from my mother, and her pouted lips, and, yes,
her stubbornness. But I have my father's pink gums,
a grip that crushes walnuts, a swipe that catches flies,
and his big hands and all the benefits thereof;
things that a gentleman would not show off,

nudge nudge, wink wink. From my time to theirs
I climb a library ladder and reach for a top shelf,
or I dig deep so that our times become stairs
laced with cobweb that lead down into the self.
I am the very history that lives unawares,
or better still that thrives on blood and flesh,
both in and through me, therefore I look inside
into a well, and there's the sky trying to hide.

My parents met when my mother was a slave.
My father did not own her, she belonged
to a neighbour. He was the type who craved
something even though he had lots cloned
from it; the fact is Mother had to be brave
once she'd caught his eye, or risk a prolonged
game of hide-and-seek with one or other
of her admirers jumping in to save her;

black men who were slaves like her and proud,
too much so to watch another black woman
at the mercy of a single white man, or a crowd,
or pack of them who saw her sex as an omen
for trouble, for possession: if white, in a shroud
of mystery, but if black then the chattel of men.
There for use and abuse, impregnated
not courted, shown respect, or venerated.

She knew this by instinct and from experiences
related to her by older women who sought to school
her in how to conduct herself using common sense.
In all their tales the woman played the fool
but lived to see another day. The essence
of it meant that her life was not a tool
for some man to poke at until bored.
She could shape her future, see what it stored,

and, by some pre-emptive move on her part,
alter it to suit her dreams. A grand plan.
Alas, she was dealing with someone just as smart.
The reality panned out differently on the plan-
tation where the head could never rule the heart,
when both obeyed below the waist, no plan-
etary positions in relation to time and date
of birth in this plot, just plain old copulate.

She lay in wait for him, as he sought her,
to say, 'You are courting the Devil's mistress
if you think you can lay even a finger
on me.' But when she locked eyes with his
all he could think of was that she was there
because she wanted him, making easy this
thing he was always doing with a slave;
the polar opposite of her motive.

A simple walk from the fields to the house
along a path twisting into a grove of alders
that comes to a sudden clearing whose
light seems pooled there, for bathing, like solder
in a flame, the blue part a phoenix might choose
to plunge in, not me or you for all the
tea in Hong Kong, though on occasions I
have swept my finger through a candle's eye.

But nothing's simple, least of all her walk
determined to meet him and perhaps stop
his eyeing her up and down, his rude talk
in front of people, their gossip to top
the story, as if it were enough to stalk
her to make her his and she would drop
everything and comply because it has always
been and will always be the white man's way:

to take what he wants when he wants,
how he wants, to go where he pleases
when he wishes, to be everything we can't
be except during the nightly release
offered by dreams when he becomes the ants
under our feet, he eats crumbs from our feast.
'Welcome to Slavery,' the sunrise would shout
before the light of that dream was out.

Dear reader, what happened next has happened
countless times, will happen countless more.
Let the record show, for too few are penned,
that he grabbed her and called her a whore.
That she fought him but he had her hemmed
in against a tree, he had done this before.
He knew what to do to make her scared –
he made the deep impression of a scar

by pressing the knife on her face. She turned rigid,
wooden, and he mounted her and he rode
flat out as she shut her mind down to get rid
of him in her and made herself a lifeless board
under his weight, his teeth biting, his rancid
breath, his hips, its thrust, its sudden load,
the knife threatening to break her skin,
so she had to, she had to, let him in.

She kept her eyes open, allowed the light
to bathe them; sun rays sunk in that grove
concertinaed through her eyes' bright
shine into her brain, already an oven
turning on a slow, steady burner the sight
of him to ashes, her hate burning to love.
Don't ask me how the worst moment she knew
switched on the best thing life can give to you.

The man may have shown more than his malice.
In the middle of lust, his knife, those bites,
something tender accidentally surfaced.
Could be because she was so still despite
everything, she spotted in his embrace
what even he couldn't see: the anthracite
inside himself, a commoner giving birth
to love's jewel, love's uncommon hurt.

He leapt off her, vomited and ran
wildly into the trees and their shade.
She wept in that clearing and sang,
whispered more like, a mother's tune made
up to soothe a teething infant in slang
known to that child, on its lips when it played.
'Hush now baby, don't cry, dry your eyes
at least you live, not cut into pieces,

but whole and alive, others see worse.'
And it went on, more a song than a prayer,
talking herself to her feet off the gorse
that was her bed shared with her ensnarer;
a shocking tune, a tune out of shock, a curse.
If her calm were a garment, then she, the wearer,
had pulled it airtight about her rattled
frame, to hold herself together though embattled.

And he, after his revulsion lessened,
knew what had hit him in the solar plexus,
but denied it to himself as if the lesson
of love only comes once we've read its prospectus,
picked a date, time, place and person
to get it on, then said, 'Love infect us!'
Ridiculous but true. He walked the town
in denial with the two faces of a clown.

One face was plastered with a loving smile,
the other, sour-mouthed and bitter-eyed.
Both flashed in equal measure all the while.
Both told the truth and yet, by turns, both lied.
His happy and sad faces, two profiles
shaped by his bones, painted on skin – two sides,
same coin, squeezed his heart for love, spun
his brain for hate: his skull hurt, his chest burned.

At night he slept facing a blank, black wall.
A large fresco painted from a dark palette
covered ceiling and floor, skirting and all
that wall; as he slept it papered the garret
that was in his head. Knowing the face so well
he tried to name it but he couldn't collect
letters to form a name he didn't have
to fit a face the wrong colour to crave.

He couldn't sleep. He couldn't look at the four
walls. He flung himself outside for air
only to come across a shadowy figure
out in the open to catch what they shared,
what everyone has to, never mind their stature,
what's free and bountiful, thin and spare,
mountain-high, pollinated and river-thick
valley-deep, our fuel and oil-slick.

What could he say? What would she do? She looked
at him. He walked up to her. At arm's length
she reached up and slapped his face. He hooked
her arm behind her and asked her as his strength
drained from him if he was the only one snooked
by this feeling. 'What?' She feigned puzzlement.
She wanted him to spell out what he felt,
but her arm hurt and water began to melt

her eyes. He turned her round to face him
and quickly kissed away each little spill
and, for each drop, a peck and with that rhythm
more tears flowed mounting these feelings until
she was lying on him and his back this time
on furze, holding her, and she with his full
cock in her hands, feeding the hardness of a stranger
into her without thinking about the danger.

Her lips on his, their tongues lapping up
each other's saliva and if those tongues
could be seen they'd be two writhing cup-
snakes trying to make a reef knot, but their lungs
need air so there's the shortest pause to suck
on the evening breeze before that lunge
for each other, each a meal with the other's name,
both still hungry for more of the same.

Not thinking about diseases – though those are rife.
Nor white redress; a sickness in itself.
Nor black despair over their woman's life:
hijacked because the heart is just an elf
next to history; persuaded by a knife,
her raceless heart fell into love's delf.
You sink or swim once you're in that drink.
No time to wonder as you wander, nor think.

How long they lay there it's hard to say
with any accuracy. Dawn started to creep
around the edge of dark so that the day,
a hint, no more, brought a similiar seep
of definition to bodies the blue and grey
night had welded to one solid mass of meat.
What was delineated by this first light?
Two intertwined bodies; one black, one white.

Enmeshed arms and legs, her head settled
on his chest. Come closer on tiptoe
and see how her head bobs, very subtle
that lift, as he breathes in and out slow
in sleep, a deep, calm sleep, untroubled
by life, all their features soft, soft as snow;
soft as ash risen from a fire, that winds
back down to earth having ridden the winds.

This is the nature of sweet transgression:
after the fact bodies become solicitous;
black and white locked in illegal passion
throw away the key, to be felicitous
until woken by the tintinnabulation
of dawn, then untangling viscous
limbs fast as if to undo the night
they've spent glued, mimicking daylight.

They stood apart, glanced about, backed off
in opposite routes; he to his room
in the big house, she to her hayloft
stacked with hay. By rights he'd be her groom
in some still imperfect future, tough
but fair. Not in this past, whose web a broom
gripped by a reforming hand will sweep from sight,
though it looks precious in this early light.

One's oppression carries with it the seeds
of liberation, some frailty or hairline fracture
cohabits with that which we most need
to free ourselves from, a crack in the armature
invisible to untrained eyes, that feeds
on our discontent and gives it imprimatur:
that night between those two was such a thing;
a song and dance for flesh and bone and skin.

She lay on her stomach with her knees bent,
her crossed bare feet swaying, pieces of straw
plaiting in her neat hands in an absent-
minded fashion, but not idle: she saw
those plaits as them under last night's big tent
punctured by stars, the two of them raw
from all that loving, all sweat and goosepimples;
when at long last they slept, those punctures twinkled

and healed into the walls warped and elastic,
yielding to dawn, dawn highlighting the dew
in their matted hair, those fixed, plastic
smiles of their sleep; like a newlywed
couple they dozed until light tried to lick
the dark off them for the salt and woke the two.
At this point her fingers untied the plait
so that she had the separate strands back.

She saw her fate in her fingers and thumbs,
turned onto her side, stood and kicked stack
after stack of hay down, pushed and rammed
herself into them, emptying the barn of racks
of pigeons until people came running from
all quarters only to see her and drop back
to a safe distance, afraid of what they saw
and who they saw doing it, knowing what it was.

They had spoken about the thing, not to bring
it down on her head but to talk it out of existence.
The man wanted her bad, a fact staring
everyone in the face. She dismissed their nonsense.
They hoped it would die down with his string
of women on two plantations to satisfy his senses.
Now they judged their jokes and whispers a curse
driven into her, that could not be reversed.

Their talk filled her up to overflowing.
She's gone mad (they thought) as a result.
She looked like she could take their goading
the way she flicked her dress at their insults
and walked with her head held high loading
that very barn with bales of hay past sunset;
except for lunch when she went for a walk,
returned morose, worked but did not talk.

No one confirmed they had seen her last night,
the bales were brought in well after insects
settled for particular oil lamps. By eight
most folks were too shattered to inspect
who was present, who absent, they bolted straight
for the kitchen caked in dirt, physical wrecks
asleep before their heads hit those straw sacks,
the day melting off their bone-weary backs.

He should have left her hanging on a limb.
Not picked her off as if she were a lime.
He forced himself under her green skin.
Ripened her way before her proper time.
He filled her head and heart solely with him.
Her flesh aches for his touch and will emit
his smell should she fail to fight and defeat
the spell of him in her with her own sweat.

This is the love that is promised the young:
a call for the body, heart and soul,
sent out on the air waves in every pop song;
answered by green hearts with only one goal –
to meet their prince charming, ride off at dawn
(or is it sunset?) and live in a castle with a moat,
dropping a drawbridge to everyone's surprise
when they exhaust all their basic supplies.

Her love did more damage to her body
than all the lyrics in all the pop songs slammed
together have done to a sentimental boy
or girl in suburbia on a diet of MTV jams.
To them a broken heart is a broken toy,
their tears happen thick and fast then stem
when they change the channel or answer the phone;
her heart's the one thing she can call her own.

For she is owned by others, bought and sold
by others, lives to serve them, dies the property
of another and her children will grow old
as collateral like her if they live properly;
avoiding the whip, stick and chain is their goal,
with their skin as a badge of anxiety.
Black skin, brown skin, nigger, slave,
worked from the cradle into the grave.

An overseer breezed in, glanced and issued
orders for her to be restrained; two men
tried to grab her and failed, then four used
ropes to bring her down, a slave like them,
a young woman, and they trussed
her up like a pig that had escaped its pen.
They restored the hay into neat stacks,
the pigeons came flapping, necking, back.

She lay there in her own piss and vomit,
orphaned by her trouble, in this sense:
not a single relative wanted to admit
that they were related to a nuisance
with a penchant for drawing static
to herself and anyone near, ever since
she blossomed from a clean stick of a girl
into a blooming woman of the world.

Guess who showed up at that very moment?
You're right if you said him, if not, who else
could help her in such a predicament?
If no relation, friend or anyone close
was willing to risk sharing her punishment,
then who but him? Who stands to lose
a little sleep when the overseer rats
on him and Father reads him the riot act.

'Stay away from those niggers, they're dirty.'
'Yes Father, I promise, you have my word.'
'You undermined Overseer's authority.'
'Sorry Father, but you should have heard . . .'
'Don't give me any 'if's or 'but's Christy.'
'Yes, I mean no Father. For the third
time, forgive me. I am your flesh and blood.
Not one of your slaves or hired hoods.'

He would never have said hood, but wait,
he doesn't have to rhyme every other line.
His father continued with much more hate,
'You beat four men who were merely trying
to follow orders. You cut her loose, berate
yourself for leaving her, and beg her to find
it in her heart to forgive you while you place
her head on your lap and kiss her face.

'My son, the very thing I feared you'd do
you've gone and done. You've fallen in love
with one when all you were supposed to do
was fuck as many as you liked, not love.'
'Father, everything you say is true,
except the dirty part. Negroes love
like us and fuss like us and wash same
as us. That's why I'm proud to take the blame.'

'How dare you stand in front of me and say
such things. I will not allow you to blacken
this family's name. Leave my house today
and take her with you. And never come back.'
His father turned on his heels and stormed away.
Christy's head spun, he felt faint and fell flat
on his face on a Persian rug that cushioned
his fall and saved his face from being crushed.

The overseer stepped over him and fled.
The house slaves were still nailed to the spot.
She rushed in, pushed them aside and knelt
beside him and kissed his brow till he came to.
This time his head nestled in her lap, then she led
him from the house and they walked and did not
look back as the crowd of slaves, overseer,
his father, all stood open-mouthed and stared.

Christy and Faith staggered in an embrace,
bracing each other upright as they marched
off that plantation, each shunned by their race.
Their backs were stiff and straight as if starched
by their conviction. This was their first taste
of what they could never achieve apart:
alone, they were too weak and compliant;
together they were strong, upright, buoyant.

Picture those two if you can, arm-in-arm,
master and slave, somewhere in the middle South,
a white man and a black woman; alarm
bells sounding everywhere on their route.
Two products of two slave-owning farms
miraculously finding their way out
together. Picture them while you can
at their most intimate, most triumphant.

They reached an oak that split the road in the dark.
They held hands and stretched but could not span
the trunk. He pulled his knife and cut the bark
with their first names intertwined upon
an arrow running through a wounded heart.
Homeless, Christy and Faith, out in the open,
circling that knobbly tree unsure which fork
to shun and which to take for better luck.

What had they done? She had never been off
her farm; he no farther than neighbours' homes.
Neither had faced a night without a roof
to run to and bed to curl up in when some
romantic notion was rained out of
existence, yet here they were, abandoned,
left to their own devices, at sea on a raft
of love's raw material, about to break in half.

They both began to cry. They sat on roots
spiralling above ground from that oak tree,
the tangled roots of their confusion if the truth
be told . . . Fortune lend a hand. Intervene for me.
They are as low as you can get, two youths
against the times; two shoots, no, three,
with no real grip on earth, facing a storm
brewing on all sides and her in her early term.

Yes, pregnant. She doesn't know it yet,
that inside is not quite what it used to be,
though from her demeanour she suspects.
Call it female intuition and you would be
warm. Older women taught her to respect,
cherish and obey the signs of her body.
What she knew she grasped only barely,
unable to put it into words this early.

Help the three of them, show some mercy
if not for the headstrong adults, then the baby,
hardly a baby – though that's academic, curse me
if I'm wrong I don't care. Until the child can ably
defend himself, yes him, let my verse be
his caul, suit of armour and nursery,
that teases his skin, tickles his brain, chimes
on his soft bones to harden, ripen with time.

Lightning, thunder, and on their heels rain.
Christy and Faith cuddled under that oak,
heads ducked, ears corked as more thunder came,
their eyes squeezed as lightning practised its strokes
nearer and nearer as if taking false aim.
They cried for something to do, neither spoke.
What was there to say that had not been said?
Anyway, they thought they would soon be dead.

Just then, as another thunder clap rapped,
followed by a lightning zap, they saw a lantern
swinging towards them, drenched in that trapped
dark. How the lamp flamed despite the storm
they'll never know, but that's how it happened.
The flame drew a horse and cart near, and firm
in his seat though wet to the bone was a man
not seen before, who would not give his name.

He told them to hide under a tarpaulin:
'Listen all you like but do not show
your faces, no matter how appalling.'
They snuggled among farm implements – a hoe,
a pickaxe, ropes, nails, a new paling
to repair a fence, leg-irons, a horseshoe.
Under the dark, they grew concerned the rain
drumming the tarred fabric and drilling the brain

might soak and drown them at their weakest;
the old devil deliver them to their enemies;
and, like two potatoes in their jackets,
lightning strike them into instant meals.
Right? Wrong. Lightning preferred a diet
of trees to some black and white meat.
You can tell from the thunder in its belly
whether lightning fooling or hungry really.

The old man spoke above the rain and thunder
adding his voice to the lightning until element
and man were indistinguishable under
tarpaulin, yet they heard what he meant
them to understand making words redun-
dant. 'Let's say for the sake of an argument,
you're on a train that no one off it can see.
What's to stop us driving till we are free?'

'Whatever you may be, don't take advantage.
We are at our lowest, at your mercy.
If what you say is true, then your strange
face is blessed and we are bound for glory.'
Faith continued, 'I am drunk on the image
of us two in some colour-blind country
I'd only dreamed about before now,
knowing in sleep it had still to be won.'

All night they drifted in and out of sleep.
Sometimes the cart wheel hit and climbed a stone,
jolted them alert and they wanted to peep
but dared not and the rhythm of the horse soon
sent them off again; other times they heard deep,
harsh voices against the old man's soft tone,
and he'd reach in beside them, quickly grabbing
a hoe, shovel or nails and strike a bargain

and they'd move on. Sometimes as they nest-
led they grew warm, then hot and manoeuvred
their hips and the swaying cart did the rest;
their prison became a love-nest; they recovered
after a little involuntary rest
only to love again, be in that groove
once more, bring on the sweet funk of lovers.
It was a case of, 'Roll me over in the clover . . .'

They wheeled into a barn edging a town
whose chorus of cocks balanced on gates,
fences and posts cock-a-doodled or crowed.
The town ruffled its feathers and stretched awake,
or sun lengthened its tongue and lapped the dew,
or both. A farm worked by hands that take
home a wage at the end of the week, not slaves.
A couple greeted them and said they were safe.

Their four children were still asleep upstairs.
Christy and Faith washed from buckets the wife
filled at the well, while the husband prepared
his specialty. They caught a whiff
that led them to a laden table. They stared.
Their mouths watered and would have dribbled if
they hadn't swallowed. Barley with honey steeped
in goat's milk, coffee, and honey on crepe.

They'd not tasted anything like it or ate
as if they hadn't, loving those two kind stran-
gers, not looking up till they had clean plates
and then only to throw heads back and drain
cups dry. Their hosts insisted they'd wait
on them, filling their plates again and again.
At last they sat, clasped hands and said grace;
shame shone on Christy's and Faith's face.

The humbled pair fell to their knees and prayed.
They were so loud the four children came down
with the youngest on the eldest's hip, all wide-eyed,
ready for the emergency they had grown
up with warnings to expect night and day,
for harbouring runaways in their home.
From their parents' smiles they realised
this was a good day, not to fear but relish.

They could smell the hot barley and boiled milk,
see the fresh bread and cheese on the table,
saw too the strange pair quivering like silk
on their knees, so joined in and the house trembled
with them all crowing, announcing some guilt
in tongues not one among them could label.
All those chickens stuffed in that little coop:
Cock-a-doodle-doo! Cock-a-doodle-doo!

The old man walked in and clapped: those tongues
flew from everyone's parted lips
twice as fast as a flock at the sound of a gun.
He ordered the young pair to grab some sleep
for the coming trip overnight down-
river, as if he never needed to sleep or eat.
He dived outside and made the sign of the cross;
afraid this crowing thing might be contagious.

Prayer can be catching. Christy and Faith
found that out. The old man always worshipped
alongside some task so that his life, awake
or asleep, was one long devotion to the Spirit.
He did not talk about it. He would take
his time thinking so that when his tight lips
separated something wonderful bound to jump
out and please people, or leave them stumped.

The lovers' room was not a room, more a cupboard
two people could lie down in with a squeeze,
locked from outside, windowless and boarded
up, with floating dust that made them sneeze
louder than the heavy furniture pulled forward
to block the half-door entered on their knees.
Lodged in a wall, they listened to the affairs
in the house, so that the wall really did have ears.

If listening in darkness is a kind of muscle,
say an eyelid, as theirs surely must have been,
then it relaxed slowly over those corpuscles;
if it is skin that creeps over a fingernail unseen
that you keep pushing back to expose more cuticle,
then in that musty space, eyelids and skin
slid over wary eyes and fingernails,
as surely as dust settled on their nostrils.

Their kind of sleep was the equivalent
of bodyguards napping while on duty.
A rest with one eyelid raised like a vent,
or both like Venetian blinds not quite fully
drawn, that you can see out of but peepers can't
see in; storks on one leg, athletes on one knee
waiting for a start that never comes,
sleep you need a rest to recover from.

Yet sleep they did, something they dived towards
and surfaced from, both for the fall and climb.
Now the children played school, spelling words,
singing numbers, tables, and nursery rhymes.
Christy and Faith wanted some: she – the boy heard
crying, still attached to his sister like a limb;
he – first a girl, then boy, girl-boy, etcetera.
More than she had in mind, quite a few extra.

How would their children look? Half and half.
Which half? The right half black, the left half white.
No. The top half white, the bottom half Af-
rican. But with our features exchanged, right?
God would mix them properly, they laughed,
kissed, and did what two child-makers might.
They were all fingertips in that pitch dark,
fingertips, hungry lips, as they skylarked.

They'll come out looking like little angels.
They'll sing as sweet as these four children
playing school, and work for an honest wage
because they'll be free. They talked under
their breaths as oboists manage
by circular breathing to hold a strain.
They held and held these thoughts and dozed,
just like the notes the musician does.

Fresh bread nuzzled them awake. Faith blinked
herself back to her name but couldn't remember
where she was and who she shared the sweet stink
of love-making with in this dark chamber.
Then she smelled dough and it made her think
to reach out and touch him just as he endeavoured
to touch her. Both screamed and shouted their
names, laughed, hugged and dragged on baked air.

Dust, thick as snuff, made them sneeze volleys.
Furniture groaned, lamplight, the colour of butter,
spread evenly on their faces, they could not see.
Their outstretched hands were taken, and muttered
words seemed to melt the coins of light off their eyes.
They were led to bucket, soap and water.
After grace, they sliced the alarm-clock
bread and smeared yellow light on thick.

The old man came in. They faced their hosts.
The husband spoke, 'You don't know where we live,
keep it that way; you don't even know us –
that's good if you get caught. All that we give
is given freely. We worship Christ.
We are repaid doubly if you believe.'
They hugged them and the children and left.
Sadness filled the spaces in their chests.

How can sadness fill the spaces inside
when they have all their lives ahead of them?
That came from the direction of their guide
who had his back and a few feet between him
and them. It sounded like the wrong aside
at the time, a ruse passed off as wisdom.
Christy and Faith held hands and fought that hurt,
the other side of love, love's other truth.

A path across two fenced fields sloped
down to a bank; fireflies' phosphorescence
detonated soundlessly in tropes,
incomplete news, some phoney essence
about following light with the letters lopped
off in careless hieroglyphics of nonsense.
The old man might have said this for their benefit,
but knew they would never believe it.

A girl not so long ago, Faith had chased
fireflies when they lit up, and stopped lost
when they left an afterglow and her poised
for another to light up and chase and lose.
Christy sat and watched them write and erase
what they wrote and tried to trace their course;
and sometimes they came on again exactly
where he'd guessed their likely trajectory.

The old man had seen many like these two.
Starry-eyed, they walk blind into the arms
of trouble. His comments aimed to douse
that light a little, make those eyes perform
seeing again. He wanted to call a truce.
Policing love felt bad, but there was harm
ahead, not the soft glow of their eyes' shine,
but dangers in front, dangers lurking behind.

They waded in cool stockings to a canoe,
no, a boat, untied it, climbed unsteadily aboard.
All this with the river gushing current news
of itself at them. The old man blubbered
instructions, or so his talk sounded, diluted
with water. What they couldn't do he cajoled
them for, how youth was wasted on the young
because they lacked the necessary wisdom.

One by one they settled in the boat in a row:
the old man (who shall remain nameless) sat
where the captain and guide should, at the bow,
Faith behind him and Christy at the back.
All had paddles. When they started to row,
no, paddle, the old man launched into his row that
castigated them for not learning how.
What a disaster, he said, to find out now.

He ordered them to put down their paddles,
to stop them doing more harm than good.
He did all the paddling, most of the gabble
was his, answered by water slapping wood.
His captive audience got an earful;
''Tis the old who are misunderstood,
not the young. The old have experience.
We know. We went through life's events.'

They tried hard not to look at each other
by studying water. Even in the dark
they knew, if their eyes met, laughter
would blurt out, break the old man's heart,
rock and capsize the boat, *Freedom*, for sure;
so they studied the keel cutting the river apart.
Still, the old man's voice cut clean through;
'I may complain but I love what I do.'

The river was not the black, blank screen
they expected. They saw flickers of current,
mostly imaginary, barely seen,
and odd shimmers, something iridescent,
spasmodically revealed, when the machine
of a shoal changed direction without assent;
or the river tried to find a cozy
position in its mineral jacuzzi.

The river bared its back to the keel
making its incision. The river knew,
as the keel made its cut, that it would heal,
heal without a scar, heal and renew,
cure and remember how the wood feels
hard as stone, and how a stone is reduced
by water to dust, then less than dust;
that's why water turns the other cheek for us.

Exactly as fireflies strafed the skin
of night with scraps from an illumined book,
so too Christy and Faith skimmed
their past to fathom how their future looked.
The part played by light was easy to think
about – that was their love, their good luck;
the dark was all the things they did not know,
and all the things they did not want to know.

They saw a swinging lamp, a faint stroke
of light ahead. 'I see, I see,' he said,
'a giant firefly.' His one and only joke.
They laughed longer than they should, as if paid
to, they didn't mean to, suddenly soaked
by surprise. They could see the back of his head,
not his smile. He steered towards the bank
and the growing brilliance of that lamp.

Tentacles of light stretched and danced
across the water, latched onto the boat
and hauled them to the shore, entranced
by the promise of a nude flame and roped
to that written-on-water covenant,
to the rhythm of the old man's deft strokes:
whatever promise a single light holds,
it drew them from the night-struck world.

The old man moved his head from side to side
trying to see behind the flame's blind screen.
He staved his paddle and whistled a code
that sparrows flick across back yards – three
quick trills – then paused and cocked his head
as birds do, fully expecting the right re-
ply. None came. His body ruffled, he tried
again, the same three, slower this time.

He dipped his paddle, much like putting on
a vehicle's handbrake, except he hoped
not just for a sudden stop – for no
bird-call came back – but to throw the boat
into reverse. He shouted, 'Row! Row!'
Christy and Faith grabbed each other then both
paddles and attacked the muscled water,
splashing, banging, digging for buried treasure.

Ground that gives, soil that falls and lifts.
Roots can't be put down, stakes can't make a claim.
A world on water, hardly a world, a shifting
world. The boat wobbled. The blinking lamp
advanced, a burning oculus sifting
the dark, its sprinkled rays breaking the clamp
of night around the river. Faith and Christy
in a crisis, invoked the name of Christ.

Darkness sprouted arms and legs, or the trees
uprooted from the water's edge and waded
towards them, or the river scrambled into these
figures from all around. The old man made
the sign of the cross. Faith screamed. Christy froze.
When darkness tears to the sound of the afraid,
when the voice peels the skin off the night
in a single blast, by mustering all the weight

of the body, the lungs must crumple
robbed of air, and burn from that brittle groan
whose deafening flare vacuums the lungs' ampoules.
Last thoughts calcify in the brain's catacomb.
The music of the blood stops stringing along, pools
and turns sour. Each pore on the skin welcomes
a long needle. The skin contracts and glistens
around the jaw. Blood fills the ear, blood listens.

Eyes lose grip on things, drain and dribble
in darkness lacerated by a thousand stars.
Something under the skin bursts in the middle
of the forehead and emits a bantam charge.
The old man shouted, 'Ambush!' His paddle
rises to strike the dark and his voice starts
other voices shouting: the boat wobbled
again, spilled all three, the water gobbled

them up. The lovers had never learned to row,
the old man had never learned to swim. The hungry
river took him in. Even as he went down
he seemed to wave twice at them to hurry
from the noisy surface, not to follow
him but escape and somehow carry
on where he left off. So they swam
for the far bank, scrambled ashore and ran

and did not stop until both dropped, weak,
breathless and stunned over the old man's fate.
Only a while ago they had moaned as he spoke
in his knowing way about the shoddy state
of youth today and how shabbily they treat
the old who were reservoirs of what was great.
Now the river filled his mouth, nose and ears;
now his silence, his absence, became theirs.

They picked their way gingerly through the trees
careful to keep the river as a wide margin
of error on their left. Passing for nocturnal species
they were two pairs of wide-awake eyes shining
with fear, with flight, not fight, as their sole lease
on life. They found a rickety shelter and barged in,
found a corner and lay down arm-in-arm
too tired to care who might own this old barn.

With a little effort they might have wondered
why it housed fresh straw, why it was falling
apart yet still seemed held together. Under
the circumstances, their oversight is not galling
so much as endearing, though it endangered
them unnecessarily and would prove appalling.
But for now they slept like two overworked oxen,
slack jaws guzzling the barn's mildewed oxygen.

What if I said they shared the same dream,
but from each other's point of view?
Would you raise your hands and scream?
Would you give up on me and on them too?
The fact is they both conjured the same stream
shallow enough for the old man to pull through.
Not deep water with an all-embracing tide
that grabbed the old man and swept them aside.

And they woke at the same moment, the point
when the old man reappears dry and cheerful.
They are so happy they embrace him, he in front,
she behind. The old man returns their hug, careful
not to hold it too long; even in their joint
dream, he's still the old goat they care for.
They woke and men were standing over them
with pitchforks trained mostly on him.

This is not for the faint-hearted. If you are,
skip this page and the next, but let me tell
you what you'll miss: the complete avatar
of what is bad and mad, and what is evil;
unspeakable acts perpetrated for
revenge, experiment, even the thrill
of it, with Christy and Faith as guinea pigs,
and their captors' humanity reneged.

Four men punched, kicked and cursed Christy,
tied him up then turned their attention to Faith
who was held down by two others as she
cursed, spat, tried to bite and fought
them. They gagged her, said she was feisty,
whooped, hollered, grunted in loud farts
through their snouts, ripped her clothes off;
all six took turns to root at the trough.

Christy pleaded with them to stop. They refused.
He banged his spinning head on the ground where
he lay writhing to be free but bound and bruised.
One of the six, after he'd done with Faith, slithered
over, aimed his tumid cock, strained and pissed
in Christy's face and told him if he bothered
them with his noise worse things would be in store
for him and her in the countdown of their lives to zero.

When the men were done, they rested, talked, joked,
revived and queued for more until they got bored.
Then they dragged them from the barn, loaded both
into the back of a cart lashed to a donkey, and drove
to town in time for an auction. Each on a rope,
one for a slave, the other for indenture; two more
bids for two different masters, one headed west
the other further south. 'I'll find you,' He promised.

He looked over his shoulder at her, she over hers
at him, till they shrunk one from the other's sight
and grew proportionately in each other's hearts
and heads. What she felt for him inside right
then cannot be put into words. Where to start,
knowing I must try for him, for her, and I might
fail? They had joined hearts, so when they split
apart, the one heart they shared, that heart ripped.

She headed west with her owner to help his wife
about the house; he deeper south. Both pined
for the other, hardly ate or slept and looked as if
they'd expire any minute. What was their crime?
They wove two threads, a black and a white life,
into one bolt of cloth shredded by their time.
Faith and Christy reached beyond their skin.
The law said no; the church – their love's a sin.

Faith spoke her thoughts aloud and who was there
but me to hear them? Her talk stilled me inside
from my usual swivels, kicks, thrusts at her.
I froze at the sound of her voice and inclined
to the nearest wall of her belly and stuck my ear,
and found my thumb for comfort when I cried.
Her words washed over me, caked me in balm,
I soaked and thrived in their sonorous alarm.

Faith was also sick for reasons closer to home.
Morning sickness, bleeding and stomach cramps
led her mistress to order her to get some
rest. An investment – she had initials stamped,
no branded on Faith's upper left arm: OM,
owned by Mason, her husband's family name.
She paid doctors to examine her property,
and found her interest had grown already.

Doctors, because each diagnosis Mrs Mason
didn't like led to their replacement, all said
the baby would have to be cut from Faith soon
or both she and the child would be dead.
Faith was bleeding. The placenta, like a moon
in front of the sun, blocked the cervix; the baby's head
knocked on the door of what would be
its beginning and its end unless cut free.

'Do nothing and both mother and baby perish;
operate and the baby will certainly be safe;
but the forfeit, the give and take, the big risk,
is that already weak mother's poor life,'
Faith heard the doctor tell the pained mistress
who told Faith about her supreme sacrifice:
there was a chance for her but not for it, with-
out the knife, and a chance for it, not her, with.

With hardly a pause, Faith said, 'I want my baby.'
But the mistress said, 'I want you. There are always
other children to be made, but you, my dear lady,
you're one of a kind. Unlike the usual slave,
you don't lower your eyes or bend your body.
Your back is straight, you look right into my face
and manage to show me the right amount of respect;
you strike a balance that is not easy to get.'

'If what you say is true dear mistress, then do
me the honour of granting me my one wish.
In the short time that I have served you
if as you say it has been well, grant me this:
let my baby live, not me. My life up to
now has been empty, quite meaningless.'
Faith then told her about Christy, their union,
journey, capture, torture and separation.

Mrs Mason cried and gave Faith her word
that the child would be reunited with its father.
She promised that as long as she lived the cord
between the baby boy or girl and mother
would be extended to include the indentured
Christy, to reel him in, bring him back to her
through her child's life with him. In their love,
Faith would be happy in the hereafter above.

The doctor took this as his cue to apply
the handkerchief soaked in ethyl oxide
over Faith's nose and mouth. Her supple
mouth with its slight pout and thick lips fixed
in a smile turned darker and a little purple,
her round face and dimpled chin relaxed,
Faith's eyelids drooped but left some white
still showing. Mrs Mason pushed them tight.

The doctor made an incision from her navel
down to her pubic hair line, the abdomen
gave way to the uterus which opened a well
of blood and amniotic fluid viscous as semen,
and there was this little body, this snug jewel
of a child, folded like plaited dough in a pan,
about to rise, rise, rise and take
up its place in the world of white and black.

Mrs Mason gawked at me and made four
rapid signs of the cross. Her right hand sped
from one point to another as if unsure
whether to open her blouse, scratch her forehead,
or touch both breasts, all in the one gesture,
carving a barrier between us. Then she said,
'Teeth in a newborn bring bad luck – pull them out;
shave the little devil's head before that cord is cut.'

The midwife gripped the pliers while the doctor
steadied me. She yanked and twisted, yanked
and twisted as I bled and writhed and hollered
for mercy to spare me, if not the ivory sunk
in my jaws. I was too young to care. What mattered
more was not having my mother's breast plunked
into my mouth right away, and the grip of her arms
around me, and her smell and mother's warmth.

Next the midwife grabbed a razor and attacked
my curly, devilish-red hair. She wasn't bloodthirsty.
She merely followed orders and worked
as fast as she could to bring an end to my misery.
In thirteen deft strokes from front to back –
that made my hair grow backwards and caused me
to comb my hair in that direction ever since –
she cleaned my scalp and cleansed me of my sins.

The doctor handed me bawling to the midwife,
and cut the cord between me and my mother.
Faith's eyes opened as the doctor sewed, and lifted
both arms for me to be handed to her.
Mrs Mason nodded her assent; since my life
was hers she could do with it what she preferred.
I nuzzled instantly on Mother's warm chest.
I felt her arms squeeze me. I felt blessed.

Maybe my mouth clamped onto some sweet
part of her and I went quiet, lay contented,
listened to her heart, soaked-up her squeeze.
I fancy she said the name Mrs Mason consented
to me having and I knew it was mine to keep,
as I had grown accustomed to her movements,
heart and voice in the seven months I developed.
But as I listened and sucked, that heart stopped.

Her arms went slack on me. The midwife prised
them off, pulled me away and as I bellowed –
startled by the sudden silence in Faith's chest –
wrapped me tight for comfort in rough calico,
swung her body, and me with it, from side to side
and sang a senseless ditty with me swallowing
on her little finger stuffed into my orifice;
hushing the beneficiary of Faith's sacrifice.

She died that I might live. A mother's gift
of life to her son doubled from one life to two:
the end of hers, the start of mine. A shift
of life from mother to son. The mother who
could easily have said no to a baby lifted
from her insisted on giving up her youth.
Faith, I breathe for me, I breathe for you;
my life is less mine and much more yours.

Mother, you were seventeen, no longer a girl,
barely a woman, though you acted like one.
You were snatched early from this world.
You left me behind, your love-child, your son.
I feel like an unfinished, imperfect pearl
filched from its shell and sold at auction.
I feel all this and know that the reason why
I live is because you, Mother, chose to die.

I do not want to live with this knowledge.
I want to lie in your arms in a casket
deep in the ground like the Mason's silage
covered by earth's tight, heavy blanket.
I want to press my ear to your soft chest
and, even if I heard nothing, I'd give thanks
that we were united in death and able
to honour a love that wasn't negotiable.

But Mother, you are dead, dead, dead.
I talk to you and you don't, can't reply.
I want to ask you if it's true what I heard:
that in order for me to live you had to die.
The servants say it and Mrs Mason said
it to me once in anger, how she would be
better off with you instead of me, how
your death was a waste for this spoiled sow.

She called me, a boy, 'Sow', and 'Sow' stayed
with me among everybody on the plantation.
I was a sombre child, morose, sour-faced.
No mother and no father to speak to anyone
about, I sucked on my thumb and paced
up and down all day long with my head hung
for all the world to see that woe was me,
I was without a mom and dad, have pity.

This pug-nosed, pout-mouthed, skin-and-bone
child has seen plenty. His head may appear
empty but his heart is full, full of his place alone
in the world, his mother dead, his father nowhere
to be seen, his race neither black nor white but some-
where in between and therefore neither.
Mrs Mason let him call her Mother;
Mr Mason would not let him use Father.

Mrs Mason taught me how to write and read.
She said my mother went straight to heaven.
She showed me where the body was buried.
Her eyes were failing and her rheumatism
twisted her fingers; my hand would be her reed,
with my child's eyes replacing her lack of vision.
This saved me from a life of slave labour;
I'd be freed when she went to her Saviour.

I asked her to tell me as much as she knew
about my father. His first name was Christy,
no title to his name, he was disowned, he grew
his red hair in a drape. His surname was a mystery.
He fell from a great height when he threw
in his lot with Faith. Indentureship in Charity,
Virginia and a journey south disappeared Christy
off the face of earth without trace like a mist.

I loved Mrs Mason. A childless marriage
made us all her children, young and old
alike, man and woman, regardless of age.
A slave pleased her if he or she never told
a lie and worked hard for their food and lodg-
ings, but God help the slave who was so bold
as to earn her displeasure: she'd work that
slave to the bone and never give her favour back.

So I was open with her like a blank book.
She wrote on my green pages all the things
I should know about the world that took,
she said, a lifetime to know, only to fling
all that wisdom accrued over years, lock
and key, into the grave. That's why God's king-
dom must exist, otherwise life makes no sense;
all this suffering without recompense.

I learned to stay out of her husband's sight
as he stamped around the house with me
scurrying from the mere sound of him; a parasite
needing the host and prey to the host; a flea
picked off his body and eaten in one bite
to get back the sustenance taken for free.
I was not a slave but I was not free. My time
was my own but Mr Mason owned me.

To him all slaves were lazy, a miracle
that any work got done and he wasn't ruined
financially. He said free labour was the axle
of the economy, not Slavery which was ingrained
in the country but whose wheel would buckle
and break since, in time, it was destined
to hit a rut in the road of economic progress,
or some similiar Gordian digress.

The few times I ran into him he held
me by the scruff of my neck and asked
who I thought I was and when I replied,
'Christy Mason, Sir,' he chased me and kissed
his teeth and shouted after me that I lied
and sucked in more air in his loud disgust.
The times he chased me with a whip I'd run
screaming and hide behind Mrs Mason.

'You don't know who you are because, young
man, you're nobody, neither black nor white!
You occupy a no-man's-land! You belong
nowhere! You've no place to go! We don't quite
know what to do with you, so nothing's done!
Your father wouldn't know you if he walked right
into you! Nor your mother! You're not to blame,
but I hate you carrying my surname!'

I should say at such times Mr Mason
was drunk. His tirade doesn't hurt any less.
I wish the wax in my ears would harden
into a lump of lead, a helmet that repels
words shot at me by him. Ah, to face him,
not run; no longer the thin child that trembles;
who hides behind his mistress's ample skirt
and shrieks like someone already hurt.

Mother and Father, I screamed blue murder
for you: two people, two races, my two halves.
Hadn't I prayed daily for my mother
to disinter if only to include me in her grave?
And seen my dad in every white stranger?
And envied children the parents I didn't have?
Thou shalt not covet . . . Yet I coveted
parents. Yearned for, ached, hungered, envied.

Wishes of mine that were never granted.
Hungers in me that never abated.
Yearnings that could never be supplanted.
Thirsts that remained unsatiated.
Covetous to the very end, haunted
till my last breath and heartbeat by that ache.
A shadow behind, in front and underneath;
some thing chasing, gaining on me in sleep.

I fought a child bigger than me who said
his father beat his mother and drank,
so I was better off without my dad.
I pummelled him till he took his words back.
I wanted a father, I didn't care how bad
he behaved. If he wanted me he ranked
highly, he qualified, I licensed him:
Holy Father incapable of sin.

My friends held my head below a pond.
One minute we were in a swimming contest
seeing who could dive underwater long-
est, the next they were calling me dishonest.
My mother was raped and I came along,
that was the truth and I should confess
and drop this love-match, love-child crap.
I would not. They panicked and let my head up.

The first time I saw my face in a mirror,
after years of looking in mirrors and seeing
not what was there but what I preferred
to be, I drew back and gasped. I saw me in
a brown face. I did not know brown before
then, only whites and blacks disagreeing.
I'd travel from one to the other and disown
myself in-between, refusing to see brown.

Mother spoke to me all the time I languished
in her belly; a voice felt underwater
and through flesh and in bone: her burnished
voice; my ear grown vestibular.
She said she was afraid that when she perished
her memories, what she called her particulars,
would disappear with her as if she'd never
lived, all erased by Death, the life-giver.

Death charges and grabs you without notice,
shrivels bodies, scrubs off all tracks on brains,
converts each ornate path and edifice
into dry-husked, thoughtless, wind-peeled plains.
Minds pile high like husks ripped with a hoarse
cry off dried coconuts till no memory remains:
the thoughts you've had, the things you've done,
perish and are lost unless you pass them on.

So she spoke. Her voice, a drum that vibrated
down her spinal column to mine, songs heard
through cotton wool; light, brittle as school slate,
bending under water; dented light that's hard,
viscous, pliable; a stick flexed out of shape
when submerged but emerging undisturbed.
My life's a brick house for death to demolish;
stories from a brick a day cannot be abolished.

Mother tells me she misses Christy, his plain,
fast talk as if words might run out, his big plans
dove-tailing with hers – two narrow lanes
blended to make one road – his curious hands
all over her, him gone leaving her skin in pain;
and some things only one in love understands.
She talked as she walked, washed, worked;
I had not lived, nor loved, but listening hurt.

Faith

Christy, you're gone from me. I press my palms
together without your clasped hands in between.
I rub back blood into my hands until warm
when it should be your hand in my one dream
that I rub the blood from and back into, no balm,
just our hands' oils, finger by finger, no cream,
down to the crinkly little bone that won't hold
still when I press and rub against the cold.

I clutch space, an ache. I press hard.
I bruise my own flesh and eat my own words.
Since you've been gone I'm beside myself sad.
I saw a sun bloom in a sky and spore
every colour of a rainbow and felt bad
because you weren't with me to see it grow.
Your absence makes a razor of that sunrise
dragged across my salt-swollen iris.

I turn my back on such mornings for you
as one would on some thing too strong to stomach
to be any good, too good to be true.
Then there are the dawns I don't see so much
as hear – voices sweet as morning dew,
but I'm too busy searching such and such
a face moving across this sunstruck country,
to mind the birds as the sun makes its entry.

I am stripped bare by the light, bare and
lonely, my bones wrung clean, the clean
bones ground to dust, scattered in the four winds;
four deserts and four lakes have opened between
you and me, the two of us at opposite ends
of a compass, poles apart like dusk and dawn,
dark and light, black and white. We share the night,
we share the day. I am black, you are white.

Why couldn't we be either one or the other?
Not both. Why fight two battles at once?
How can we be in two places and together?
But in this place at this time every ounce
of skin conspires against our love. Gather
trade-winds, let the sky fill its ample lungs,
peel off my skin. Leave just flesh and bones;
and me, raceless, like dew, trees and stones.

To slip this skin, shed it for something new,
that's no colour on earth or in the sky. Raceless
like light. And our love as lithe as a minnow
on a river, and the river all the lighter for the bless-
ing of a moon. The streets washed clean by dew,
by light. The houses painted from pillar to post
the one colour of love, which is every colour
ever seen, every colour dreamed, but ours.

I scrub, fetch, sew, wash, iron,
put wet things out, take dry things off
clotheslines, measure my days by the wrung,
beaten light journeying across the floor
in stripes, bars, wondering if your mind runs
the same way, if you do the same chores,
if you push wonder from your face, like a lock
of hair absently put behind your ear but

it won't stay there, falling in your blue eyes
again. You're not with me. You're with someone.
Somebody to keep you warm, who says, 'Yes,'
when you call love, darling, petal, woman.
You've forgotten about me. I am less
each day I'm absent, less than my name.
Absence is a wind that fans love's fire
or kills love's candle flame for ever.

I did not mean your people to despise
you for loving me. If I could rub off the black
and be like you, to be with you . . . I realise
that I can't. I am black from head to toe, back
and front, black gums, black cuticles, black eyes.
You thought me beautiful, black made you ache
for more black, so much black I turned you blue,
your white became black and I became you.

Christy, I am still your Faith. Remember.
Daily I see your face and say your name.
I hug my pillow and fool myself its straw
is your red hair and me keeping it warm
is you warming me, loving me raw,
and me hugging it no less than your arms
returning my embrace. My face in that pillow
keeps the cold at arm's-length, bans sorrow.

Can you see me as I see you? Can space
stretched between us out the light by which
our love thrives? When you conjure my face
you draw blank, a landscape filched
of trees and nothing except distance,
the faint line of a horizon; a land pinched
bare and us not there. Our thoughts bereft
of space and time until no thoughts are left.

My life stripped of you, bark off a stick,
and me stranded, woman, naked; what
a priest chops to pieces on his pulpit
caroling me as firewood to his Sunday flock
to keep them from getting burned the other six
days. Lizard skin, snake head, stink slut,
names the children call me, my own lost
in the broken heart's frigid permafrost.

My smell, my looks, my misery keep those
children a stone's throw away but not
out of earshot — a child's words whose
stones hit you soft at first as the touch
of poison ivy that's nothing, then a bruise,
or the gentlest bite of an ocelot:
she loved a white who vanished; her belly
big with his seed, her only family.

(Mother kept me as her informed witness,
safe from tongues. Whereas most foetuses
might confer a little morning sickness
on their unsuspecting hostesses,
a little bile, a touch of acid, queasiness,
I made Mother paralytically nauseous.
She thought she was dying with Christy's child
her sole proof of all her past trials.)

When I sing I mourn your absent love,
Christy. I pull my hair, I wring my hands.
I twirl the end of my skirt like a glove
round my fingers. I do not enter, I stand
in doorways, linger, when I should leave.
I hope you will walk in or out as planned.
But you're away and you stay gone, with just
the remembered smell of you to keep my trust.

The you and not you in my life, my days.
The me and no you, never able to shake off
damp and cold; in heat, my hooded eyes –
my blind to shut out the whole world of
you not here with me. I harden in ways
you – if you were around – wouldn't approve.
My skin thickens, I smell, I don't care,
I twist the knots in my matted hair.

My nails grow, curl, and turn back in
on themselves. When I walk into a door-
frame or miss the last step on a landing,
there is a hurt, a swelling, a jolt, or
a small fracture that happens to something
bearing my name, but there's no one, no her
to whom Faith sticks, no body to blame,
not even a she to answer to that name.

A child cries out, Mother! What Mother?
Who mothers? Not me. I hear a baby. I think
Baby. I'm in its vicinity. But that cry for her
means nothing to me. If it is meant
for me I am barred from answering it. I hear
misery. But I have enough of my own, thanks.
Behold need! But how can I answer
when need is my middle name, I swear.

I walk from that baby until its mewl
is a small sound, miles away, a bald bird
in dirt below its nest, the lost jewel
of a stray calf someone's bound to have heard
and will attend soon – but not this fool,
not me. Cries drown in my throat, a sword
I swallow over and over awake or asleep,
that makes my skin goose up, crawl and peel.

Christy said to me as we sheltered
under the giant oak in heavy rain
with lightning crawling as it thundered.
'My heart is full of love's dull pain,
so full, that were I to die now, murdered
by the weather, it would be germane.'
I took him to mean that death by lightning
was better than to have lived without loving.

Locked in the wall of that Quaker house
Christy sweet-talked me; 'My skin was dead,
a cover for my flesh, a faded blouse
worn carelessly, my bone-bag and bone-bed.
But with you, skin is a sensation doused
in oil and set ablaze, something to be read
with you as my instructor, my skin as text
in our skin-school of gaze, touch and reflex.'

Christy promised me a first-born daughter,
then a son followed by another girl
and boy. I replied between our laughter,
'It's alright for you to promise the world
when I'll have to carry and bear them after
your work is done.' 'And what wonderful work!'
he yelled, rolling onto me in the dark;
his legs prising my thighs further apart.

'Not you only, Faith, the two of us.
Whatever you do, I do; when you fall
pregnant we'll bear our children simultaneous-
ly.' 'Yes! Christy, let's turn with you still
in me.' So we hugged, hooked legs, pooled trust,
turned, without him coming out at all.
Christy, love fused our bodies hip to hip,
arm in arm, lip to lip, nothing else could fit.

There was nothing between us but skin,
nothing could get between us, not even
a blade of that razor dark, nor the skimmed
silence in that hiding place our uneven
breathing turned sweet then sour as sin,
or independent thinking. It was heaven
on earth, our just dessert, our big bounty,
for finding love where love wasn't meant to be.

(Love between two people from two races.
She says it as easy as day follows night,
but this is 1861 in the Confederacy.
A woman and a man, one black, the other white,
in a nation with two heads commanding one place,
each threatening to rip out the other's sight.
And all they want to do is live and love.
There's no ransom demand, no force involved.)

I licked Christy's tight tummy which trembled,
oscillated like mercury in a dish,
then shrank from my tongue. I bent my head,
kissed and in the middle of each kiss
lifted my lips a fraction off him and burbled,
'There, there, be still for me during this
examination.' And sure enough the tremor
melted; he begged me to keep up my murmur.

Who said anything about stopping? I tried
to stop but found I couldn't help myself.
Christy laid his hands on my head, sighed,
and his own head fell back and he lifted
his spine and I swung my hands behind
his waist; the moist small of his back shifted
from side to side. Again he urged me on.
As if I needed urging. I was too far gone.

As was he. The two of us slaving for the wages
of sin; consumed by touch that hungers
for more touch, that can never be assuaged.
The two of us and no one else under
the sun when we were together, our bodies
welded into one by the glue of our plunder
of sin. If that's the name you must plaster
on our love, go ahead slave and master.

This tapestry of knotted arms and limbs
cannot now be undone; two hearts strung as one
won't be unstrung. After a man climbs
high and sees beyond the horizon,
how can he settle for the flat line
presented to him as the limit when he comes
down? He views all borders as a gimmick.
He strikes out on his own to beat that limit.

Love's for displaying in life's gallery.
Love wants to show off its intricacy.
Love won't be cooped up and pilloried,
or hidden away where no one can see.
Love spreads wealth world-wide.
Love shares the secret of its alchemy.
Everybody glitters in love's clothes;
love turns us all from base metal to gold.

Christy

Christy studied his hands. First the front.
Can he read palms? A line near the thumb
breaks into tributaries that run
over the wrist but feed back to form
a curved river, bent candle, or cut burnt
in flesh, only to disentangle plumb
between index and middle finger: the river bends
fed by two mouths; the candle burns both ends.

He flipped his hands. The knuckles are gnarled,
bruised, swollen. Tendons welded to the wrist
stand in a bed of tall veins, his curled
fingers form a huge hammer for a fist.
He plants his feet and pounds a bag of marl;
boxes shadows in his new life as pugilist.
He fights at fairs and roams from country to town,
he earns his bed and board, he bites his tongue.

Between bouts, he checks each plantation
on the pretext that he's scouting the area
for new talent or better competition.
His hammer hands – always healing – are a
boxer's dream, hard and quick and numb,
but he can't straighten his fingers or draw
or write since he can no longer hold a pen.
His brain is numb. He sleeps with his eyes open.

He tastes his own blood when he swallows,
and spits what may as well be saliva.
A voice trapped deep inside him bellows
when he sees a man his age who's a slaver.
How he keeps his cool he doesn't know,
but he arranges it so the man is another
contestant to beat or be beaten by.
Win or lose Christy's the one who cries.

You can tell he's crying. There's water
spilling from the outermost corners of eyes
that were or weren't jabbed or butted, whether
he's sprawled in the ring or he defies
gravity and is the last man standing; victor
or vanquished, the one who groans or sighs.
He deals in fists for Faith, his sole ally;
his job shuts eyes and makes teeth fly.

Let's return to his capture and humiliation,
him forced to watch – as he lay tied and gagged –
Faith's serial, repeated violation
by six white men. The morning the two were dragged
to town for the slave and indenture auction
that would separate them, Christy begged
those men to fight him man to man, one by one
with their bare fists as their only weapon.

They took one look at the delicate youth,
laughed and agreed. Modest bets were laid
on which punch and how fast to knock out
the slightly crazy Christy and put him to bed
in the middle of the morning; the first uppercut,
roundhouse, jab, or hook. Nothing was said
about the second, third and fourth among
the six trying to bring Christy down.

The first stepped up and jabbed a bit as though
taking Christy's measurement for a suit
he was tailoring to bury him in. So
Christy stood, tensed, a ripe fruit
begging you to reach up it's that low.
His body shook. An entire minute
passed with this man sizing Christy up
trembling like a leaf, rooted to one spot.

What the man read as fear were fists
gripped tight till the whole hand whitened,
vibrated, nails cutting in. But Christy's
stance was wrong, square on, too tightened
when he needed to loosen a little. The first
punch to his jaw, a roundhouse swing,
knocked him to one knee. He sprang back up
only to invite another and again he dropped.

Again to one knee. This time his left buckled.
If sparrows sang nearby in the copse,
if for an instant the light of the world, suckled
from the sun, faltered (a total eclipse
squeezed into a flicker – everyone that could,
blinking at once) then before his collapse
Christy heard birdsong and saw a dark void,
Faith fading, reversing an instant Polaroid.

Christy, caught by the same awkward right,
lies fast asleep in a straw bed pictured
in his mind, as robins sing, his head light,
his knocking knees drawn up so he's curled,
his elbows tucked in at his sides. His portrait
of his darling Faith, spoiled, erased, hurled
from the cherished world into the contemptible;
the punch flicking a switch in his temple.

The right-handed man's five friends
knew he was playing. They cheered those
two lazy swings that paid dividends.
But those two taps, those casual roundhouses,
combined to skeletal keys that opened
a door behind which the comatose
Christy suddenly awoke and reared to his feet
with a leading uppercut to the man's teeth.

There was a sound of racked antlers clashing
as the bottom jaw was driven up and into
the top. The man bent way back, lashing
his arms out in a wild, grabbing motion.
His features shuffled into surprise washing
over his face and, in a rapid substitution,
a blank, glazed expression. He rocked
forward (Christy stepped aside) he dropped.

Just as timber crashes slow from high to low
he toppled out before he landed on his face.
In this spell his friends' jaws fell so
agape a fly could have cruised the space
of each mouth in turn. The hush that follows
a collective intake of air means all trace
of that fly of the moment, in one mouth
or the other, wide open, is wiped out:

swallowed by the backdraft from that gasp;
reduced to a tickle sparked deep in a throat.
The compound eyes did not foresee this last
slide into acid, the traction of a mountain goat
failing it too; the fly of fortune in a disaster
movie of its own; the masticator (great)
devoured, finished the way it flourished –
roped in for another to be nourished.

The five friends jumped in and pummelled
Christy, but the onlookers who had placed bets
wanted their money's worth fairly. They pulled
them off and asked who wanted to be next.
Christy stood rooted, the crowd swelled.
All five wanted to wring Christy's neck
for their prostrate comrade's injured pride
and theirs, caught in public and by surprise.

The loudest among them threw himself
into an impromptu, moving, square ring
shaped by spectators. A referee, self-
appointed, from the crowd, promptly stepped in.
The man launched a barrage of right and left
hooks, jabs, elbows, pokes and swings
at Christy's head and body. Christy tucked
his elbows into his side with his head ducked

behind his forearm and fists which absorbed
most of the blows. Some slammed into his ribs,
stomach, back of his head, groin and bored
him to tears, squeezed from his clamped eyelids.
For he felt nothing, thinking of Faith's ordeal
and not able to forget what those men did.
He took the hits to feel bruises on him
instead of pain radiating from within.

The man's punches became kisses sprayed
over Christy's body liberally.
Portions of Christy's attention deployed
to each bruise taking from the totality
of his mind on Faith as those six men's prey,
and him just feet away, bound to her reality.
The man ran out of breath, slowed and stopped;
Christy threw him a right and the man flopped.

Christy beckoned the third man into the ring
before the second was dragged out by his heels,
Blood gushed from a gash in the soft skin
above Christy's left eye. If he couldn't feel,
now he couldn't see from one eye. Bring
him a cloth. This came from the referee.
Christy just used his forearms to swipe
his eye, bloody nose, and split bottom lip.

The third man exercised much more caution.
But for every punch he landed, one returned
from Christy just as bruising. He drew blood from
Christy's right eye and top lip, and earned
the same. He aimed for Christy's jaw-bone,
missed, but was less fortunate. He captured
Christy's left hook squarely on his temple
(or should that be surely) and he toppled.

Christy flagged on the fourth. All applauded.
If Faith could speak would she say, Soul mate!
Do not kill yourself for me. I am appalled
that you bleed on my account. Don't dissipate
your life on them. You're no good to me mauled
beyond recognition. Live for our love's sake.
If not for you, if not for me, then live for love
that set our hearts going swift as doves?

Did Christy hear or imagine he heard Faith
implore him to live? His body hurt
but his heart ached twice as much when the fourth
man stepped up on fresh legs and, from the start,
relentless as a pendulum back and forth,
his fresh arms swung, and as accurate.
Christy's eyes closed up. He turned his back
and curled up. The man redoubled his attack.

Parts of the crowd squinted through their ten
fingers each time the man picked his spot
with an uppercut as if trying to straighten
the bent nail of Christy's body or stop
its human shape for some alteration Satan
would make or a mad potter to a bad pot.
Others cried out, cringed on Christy's behalf.
Only the man's conscious friends laughed.

They urged on their friend telling him where
to hit, choosing parts of Christy to bruise
and bloody; each blow eliciting a cheer.
The people in the crowd, no longer amused,
started to shout instructions for their
man, to save him being pulverised:
Guard your left side! Jab with your right! Duck!
Cover your ribcage! Keep your arms up!

Christy saw shooting stars with each punch
from his adversary, stars culled
from a firmament of fists launched
at him. He heard hammering in his skull,
interspersed with voices sounding like staunch
allies telling him what to do to annul
the barrage. He caught the 'Jab!' command;
curiosity operated his hand.

Sure enough he hit flesh and bone.
Again he heard 'Jab!' and threw his weight
behind his punch and heard the crunch of stone
on shell as his fist made the man's nose break.
The crowd whooped, clapped, stamped, groaned.
The man keeled over, resigned to his fate.
Christy kept on swinging blindly at the air;
the two remaining men disappeared.

The self-appointed referee pronounced
Christy the winner. The crowd cheered, hoisted
Christy shoulder high and he bounced
on the makeshift champion's throne foisted
on him, struggling to be put on the ground,
calling Faith, which the crowd mistook for a boast,
picked up and made into a chant as they
paraded him around the square: 'Faith!'

But Faith did not respond. The two returned
with legal backing and had Christy's trunk
trussed for auction — indenture — a five-year term.
The highest bidder? The referee! He'd sunk
everything into a travelling fair and had earned
money from a boxer now too punch-drunk.
Christy couldn't see. Hands washed his face,
body and led him to a quiet resting place.

For days Christy sank into nightmares:
his fists passing clean through the entrails
of six invincible men made of air;
Faith in an orgy instead of her trials.
He left town in a cart with his owner's fair.
Cuts closed. His eyes lost their scales.
He gazed at his palms' meaningless sutures;
turned to his knuckles and saw his new future.

My hands aren't mine. I'm at their mercy.
They surround my days with aches and pains.
They make me beg, pray, cry and curse
the day I was born, my race, my useless name.
My fingers curled into a fist are a purse –
leather and stones, not skin and bones. It contains
enough hurt to numb a skull for revenge;
the woman I love and lost and must avenge.

Hands listen. Don't harden against my story.
I could do nothing more to stop her loss
without embracing death and hopeless glory.
I lay bound and gagged. I could smell moss
in the hay and clay of that barn. The gory
details don't change one bit, they feel worse
with each telling: I loved, I lost, I pine;
now my only fight is against ring-time.

I sit up from a lying position with my arms
behind my head. I squat and stand with the weight
of a man balanced on my shoulders. I farm
muscles pounding a bag until the shape
of that bag for a body is a death–charm.
Then I bathe, eat, sleep and wake
for a bout, or dream the one dream I always
lose in, starring Faith walking away.

I take it easy before a match; bantam
movements, no noise or light. I pretend
Faith's return hinges on the outcome.
In my warm–up I box the air and send
the ghosts of six men into oblivion.
But they shadow me. They respond
even as I stand over the ghosts of them
to make sure they never rise again.

But they always do. Their shattered shadows
reassemble, renew and charge at me afresh.
I swivel, twist and step to catch each foe
with my fists. I keep hitting guilty flesh
and bone, even after they appear to go
down; they always return to pressure
me with what they did before my eyes;
I hear Faith cry and call. I watch them die.

They form a line. Christy's knuckles ready
themselves – both arms up beside his face,
elbows tucked into his ribs. He steadies
his nerves with slow, deep breaths; paces
himself to get through about six bodies.
The square ring is his heart's carapace.
Faith is redeemed, unscathed, in those rounds
with the hungry men that he grinds down.

At times during practice Christy weighs
nothing on his feet, his arms work like wings,
his bones feel hollow; halcyon days
when his skin traps the air and sings
with every step, twist of his trunk – a maze
of jabs, ducks, uppercuts and swings.
He felt this when he fell in love with Faith:
light and nimble as a featherweight.

He avoids mirrors, never touches his face.
No one dares to stroke his cheeks anymore.
The last hands to run over them and trace
their smooth, soft, arcadian contours
were Faith's. Now that look is scarce.
Now his skin is disfigured and coarse.
His owner dashes water on him or a slap
if a bout goes wrong and he gets knocked flat.

He takes opponents for prospecting country:
the bigger the better, plenty to explore.
When he hits them he's blasting rock to see
if there's gold, silver and iron ore –
his precious names for grades of the degree
of pain he causes them – hidden there. More
rare is plain rock in a barren place;
most have rivers with gold on the surface.

When he finds just rock he's in trouble.
All he can hope to do is make a big mess
while he avoids being reduced to rubble
himself by the same blasting process.
Trudging river banks turning pebbles,
stones and mud is child's play, painless.
When two rocks meet they always clash,
the weaker of the two will simply smash.

He envies men the calm he sees settling
on them when he knocks them numb as ice.
He tries being a passive landscape, letting
perfect strangers blast his rockface to pieces,
for some miraculous beating resulting
in sweet, vacant, celestial peace.
But his fists won't allow him to pause
from his single, unsung, solitary cause.

It's Faith he wants to find and Faith's body
restore unsullied with each redemptive bout.
This makes him unpleasant company.
Most days he fights, most nights he shouts
in his sleep; awake or asleep he's moody.
His fists are cruel, but worse things spout
from his tongue which reduces grown men
to heaps of spit and tears like children.

Christy faced a black opponent twice
his size and did not know what to do.
At first he took punches, ducked and sliced
air around the man's temples with a few
reserved swings aimed at white space,
until the man spoke. I'll be lynched if you
let me win. His red-rimmed eyes pleading.
Christy nodded and launched his farewell greeting:

a thrust below the ribs to bring the body
forward, an uppercut to send the head
shooting back, a side-step and apology
uttered to Faith more than to the untidy heap
that was a man, less than a man, somebody
owned and trained to fight and lose instead
of beat a white man, so that even in the ring,
stripped to the waist, a white face still grins.

In his fights he must be Faith's champion –
he looks for her in every black woman –
not that young man bound and looking on
while she suffers at the hands of those men,
That young man died when his fists were born.
Christy is miles from him in all but name.
He dreams about his old self with Faith,
loving each other in public and private.

He became one trembling nerve pressed
into love's service. Nothing else mattered.
There was nothing he wouldn't have stressed
for love; to secure what both hungered
for, knowing love cannot be possessed.
As long as there was life, love prospered.
Now his fists do the talking and his lips
aren't for loving, but for cursing and spits.

He was an appetite, now he can't taste
his food. His life is blood on his tongue,
head choked full of altitudinous waste.
He feels nothing when punched but numb
in his skull and chest, and rubber in place
of skin, and rocks where bones belong.
He's fluent in a circle, a ring and square
for home, with Faith gone he can't care.

Tom

The oldest piece of moon, the smallest piece,
the merest moon, guided old me away
on a moon-street, just for me, no one else
could see by or benefit from that deadly day.
A road of silver laid on water that ceased
to exist the moment I left it behind. May
I never walk another road like it in my life.
I could hardly breathe, I was scared stiff.

But it made me live. All around me darkness
thrived. I heard men's voices, saw lamps
put out paler, shorter roads in the blackness.
Grey shadows stumbled, tripped and fell on stumps
of that dark which absorbed the starkest
noises, muffled the men's voices to grunts,
complaints, curses; but the river divided,
sweeping off the young lovers whom I guided.

If the moon worked for me, why not for them
as well? They saw a path of their own
from the same moon – one that could stem
the tide – and escaped. They did not drown.
They couldn't paddle but they could swim.
I can't stay afloat but I could out-row
the devil himself if I had to do it.
The moon on that river made me dote.

I somersaulted under water, immersed
myself in the element that's my sign,
and should have died then and there, but first,
so I kept telling my water-numbed mind,
I had to save that couple from the curse
of race in our colour-warped time;
take them above the thirty-ninth parallel
to a safe place far from the race peril.

Is there such a place on this good earth,
I hear you ask, almost immediately.
I say, even if there isn't, it's worth
pursuing; even though for blacks lately
things have gone from bad to worse.
I remember I was created free.
I lift my head to the moon with this memory,
my illuminator, my Saint Gregory.

Icy fingers on an ice hand, several
hands, dozens of fingers, underneath
my skin, gripped my bones, my vital
organs, and squeezed out all the warmth
in me. I revolved while the current revelled
in my despair. I wrestled with death
on that river-bed, not knowing I'd made
the shallows by the bank and was unscathed.

I lifted my head clear of the icy hands
around my throat, over my eyes, ears;
drew a deep breath on icy air and
garnered my hopes, hemmed in all my fears,
braced myself for capture by those brigands.
I am old, I have lived, I said, all geared
up to die on the spot in the dark, wet,
cold; but my time hadn't come as yet.

I could be bait for fish now, water
in my lungs. My flesh scraped off the bones,
the bones stripped of their marrow after
the current has sucked them smooth as stones.
I saw my porous bones break and scatter
far from what was once their home.
The river put its lips to my ears and hissed
I should resign myself to its wet kiss.

But I thought of that fragile, young couple
in love, how much they needed me now
after we'd gone through all this trouble
together. To lose when we'd nearly won;
have everything come to nothing; buckle
under the first major test we'd known –
not if I was true to my name. I pushed off that
river-bed and crawled to the mud flats.

Think of all the other couples who would
find themselves by a cedar or oak tree
in a thunder-storm at night, hungry and cold
and no knight in his chariot harnessed to a steed
to come along – since God broke the mould
when he made me – and rescue them free
of charge. Paid by the bounty of their happiness;
annoying the hell out of white supremacists.

Think too of the children born with Slavery's
cord wrapped three times round their necks;
a cord I want to cut to set them free
in the world, not have them writhe like insects
trapped on a web, in gum, by a sudden freeze,
deliberately turned on the shell of their backs;
they're not my flesh and blood but everybody's;
love and lust fills the world with babies.

I want to undo Slavery, cut the string
so those children breathe air, lead them
to a place where they can grow strong,
walk upright, heads held high as heaven,
throats filled not with cries but a song,
so even though they are hungry, thin as stems,
they know they are free, they put down roots,
blossom into trees, offer me shade and fruits.

That night the river ripped off my clothes; my wet,
naked, wrinkled body was left exposed
to the cool moon and cooler stars which kept
their usual distance. I hugged a tree and froze
as the lamps fell on me and their carriers stepped
feet from me and took my skin for bark, my nose,
shut eyes and closed mouth for the very tree
I held onto for dear life as they trampled by me.

I thanked the tree, the dark, the moon and God
for sparing me. Their ghostly voices faded.
Lucky for me they'd come without a dog,
or else I would have been sniffed out and made
minced meat of: too old to fetch a hog's
price at an auction; too old to learn a trade;
an old dog who can't be taught new tricks;
too weary to be stirred by the whiff of a bitch.

But enough of that 'old' stuff. I use it rather
than have it use me. It pays to stoop,
move slow and appear dumb. Others
think better of you. You make them look
good. Their faults pale to trifling matter
next to yours. They like you to group
near: they talk to you as if you can't
hear; they need you to act compliant.

They tell you things so basic you have to laugh,
but to yourself; laugh and carry on the work
for freedom. You can show a horse the trough
but you can't make it drink. At that fork
in the road that young pair witnessed enough
rain, thunder, lightning and bad luck
to last for life. When they glimpsed my lamp,
they jumped at their first chance to decamp.

An old head with a young heart in a not
so young body, I drive a cart along a trail
hoping to bump into a lost soul or two out
in the middle of nowhere, chasing some holy grail.
I find them or they find me, mostly, but
if we don't, it's hunting season and they're quail.
I hear them in the caterwauling wind,
the lightning whip, the rain with its sting.

Either you're with me or against. Do I care
that my cart, my argument can't carry
everyone? I do what I must. What are
my critics doing to help? They pass airy
judgement on me. I've gone much too far
now with this thing to begin to worry.
I cherish the people I meet. This is no ploy:
nothing beats their faces peeled with joy.

All I do is plough a road with a cart and horse.
I can row a boat through rapids but I can't swim.
I go with those I help from house to house.
When a man stops me to rob me, I barter with him.
He lets me go. After all, I am seen as use-
less; not worth the effort of a cutlass swing.
Transporter of straw and a few tools,
I am taken for one of those dying old fools.

He sees a wrinkled man who has had his life,
not me. I am not finished with living –
there are things I have to do – even if
life is through with me. I dream of giving
the rest of my days to a cause that's a wife
to me in the sense that I'm married to saving
souls and want no more from my body
than a decent shot at eternity.

Once I was a furrow in a cotton field,
dawn at my back, sunset on my forehead.
My spine curved towards the soil's soft yield
in benediction, toes ploughing into red
earth, my body a knot, one long ache I feed
with every move and can't move unless fed.
From the moment I wake until I snatch
a little numbing sleep, I am that ache,

that ache is me. My head nearly empty,
for the sake of emptiness. My ears beat
with my blood and whispers; hearing plenty
they try to hear nothing. My eyes speak
my mind and ignore my heart's entreaty;
eyes bulbous with pressure and opaque.
Sometimes light clamps my skull and everything
I see is run through by sheet lightning.

Eyes hooded against those lovely and stark
mornings and noons, lids swollen-cried,
dragging my stranger's feet through earth
until my spine curves and I hear nothing inside,
not my breath, not even my hollow heart,
nothing but furious blood amplified;
bent back bearing down, down, down,
to deep below the welcoming ground.

Could I see all this the day I walked from
the plantation, bled like me, of its fecundity?
When did I allow the thought to form
that I must leave or die trying? I felt dirty
just for having that thought, but it wormed
its way back into my brain with impunity.
The million bolls of cotton ready for picking
shone in the moonlight and were unblinking.

Hadn't I grown old in these very cotton beds?
I knew them better than anything under the sun.
How far would I get with feet heavier than lead,
with a back that had dried in one position?
Spared the overseer's whip because of my grey head,
what more could I ask? I walked in one direction.
I didn't look up or down once I left that field.
Day collapsed like a tent. My eyes peeled.

I marched into and through a cloying drape,
always into and through it, feeling silk and brick
consume me, stifled with each step, wrapped
in gauze even as my forehead pierced fabric.
My eyes sore from staring. When did I drop?
Did the dark act like a cushion and break
my fall? I saw something thicker than night;
I struggled to walk, I fought to stay upright.

Hands inspected me, turned me on my back,
twisted my face this way and that, raised my head,
fed me water hard as ice and gentle slaps
with the back of fleshy fingers to the left side
of my face. I shook off this sudden attack
of attention. After a life without affection I'd
grown accustomed to sweating off hurts,
finding comfort in a slave's comfortless work.

I was starved of a woman's touch: how
it coerces ever so gently with unwritten
promises of more where that came from. Now
I turned the right side of my face towards her ten
fingers, praying she'd use more of her know-
how to correct her neglect of it; smitten
before I opened my eyes, thinking angel
and wings and I had died and this wasn't hell.

She spoke urgently. We must get away
from the road. Her voice was deep. She dragged
her words as if hauling in bundles of hay.
Her floor-length dress was clean, not the rags
I usually smelled on another field slave.
I guessed she was about my age from the bags
under her eyes and lined skin that seemed rough;
but her face exuded kindness and love.

Both are hard to come by. Slaves banish
both or keep them hidden to get by before
both become another thing to take from flesh
that has already surrendered much more
of itself than anyone should request
or have to give of their body and soul.
At my age love dries up, leaves you a husk:
you have none to give and you don't ask.

What you don't have you don't miss much.
You bury the sting of what you're missing
in your life, in everyday tasks, just as such
things as bees get on with business and sing
despite the poison in their tail that's a crutch
and a weapon, since it kills them if they sting:
for love to survive in this woman this long,
she must have laboured all her life with a song.

Stones in her belly and a song in her throat.
Stones for a pillow but a thinking heart.
My life of two paddles and a little boat,
a willing horse and a rickety cart
began with her. She showed me the ropes.
She was the original driver. She started
the road our enemies can't walk or see down,
that joins, without a seam, Slavery to freedom.

The Underground Railroad that makes moles
of us all, made a human out of me. I think,
This is kindness, for the first time in my whole
life when she cradles my head for a drink
after mildly slapping me back to life. Her hold
warms me; stones turn to mud in my brain.
My back flattens from its usual, fixed curve;
my eyes well up and shine; I feel love.

Can I stand? Walk? I want to tell her my legs
just sprouted wings, but I am afraid or too tired
to talk. I beam at her, squint and nod instead.
We hobble into the bush, arm-in-arm as if tied
together in a three-legged race. She says
what we will do from this moment has been tried
before, that I am to trust her completely;
I nod and we continue on secretly.

She helps me into a cart, covers me and says,
'No matter what you hear you are not to show
your face.' The rest is a series of bumps, rays
from the blinking, swinging lamp that burrows
through cracks in wood whose creaks play
havoc with my nerves making my breath shallow;
the reins flicked on hide interspersed
with her clicking tongue spurring the horse.

As soon as she lets me, I grab those
reins, wield that lamp in the dark for others
who run off plantations in a daze.
My eyes settle in my head, no longer eager
to leave my skull. Once my ears froze
to the drum of my blood, now they smother
that blood with things, their music, the ear's pearls:
trees full of rain, birds filling trees, this world.

In the wet months my bones still ache.
I grind my teeth in my sleep as if dragging
my feet through mud. Sometimes I wake
and it is as though I never stopped raging
and so never slept; and Stella, my mate,
saviour, hugs and tells me to stop waging
war, I am safe, and that soothing drawl of hers
soon sends me back to dream beside her.

Stella

First things first. The second they settle
into the caulked safety of her log cabin,
the moment she unhooks him from her, she shells
him of his clothes. Armed with soap, basin
of warm water and a rag – as he pastes himself to Stella's
single bed – she dabs at all the injured places on him.
Stella, he says, Stella. Yes, she replies. Yes, Tom?
He adds nothing to her name but more of his hum.

Each find is different. She almost stood
on Tom in the dark before she saw him. If he were
a needle in a giant haystack, she would
still have found him – some homing instinct – or
walked up and down all night, such was the mood
that gripped her: a trance, her face turned more
to the stars than anything under her nose;
and there he was, face-down, in a death-pose.

Off comes road dirt from his neck, ab-
domen, thighs. She changes the water twice.
His joints are seized rigid. Each dab
applies pressure to his joints. He winces.
They loosen and relax to receive her rag.
She touches the curve in his spine, gives it a nice
scrub and it arches for more contact.
The water's clean but she says, I'll be right back.

Do not let his key come near your lock,
she thinks, as she refills the basin. Old woman,
she lip-syncs, You have read this book
before. You know he is only a man,
wanting what all men want, namely a fuck,
and next morning he'll make you understand
that he has to move on to greener pastures;
that he won't be harnessed by a new master.

Wash your hands of him as he will surely
wash his of you. Point him in the right direction
and kiss his sweet ass goodbye, don't rely
on your instinct in this instance, let discretion
rule your heart today. She says this hourly
to herself but can't resist his erection,
maintained as he sleeps and weeps in his sleep,
undiminished even though his foreskin peels.

He's lying on his back, in a dream, arms twitching,
perhaps picking cotton going by the frown.
She leaves her corner of the cabin used as a kitchen,
strolls over to the bed, brazenly lifts the eiderdown
and straddles him. He grips her waist, opens
his eyes and smiles so broad she laughs, her head thrown
back: her first laugh, his first smile, for how long
she doesn't know; time stands still; they carry on.

Carry on and rest, doze, wake and resume.
She stir-fries a meat-and-two-veg feast fed
to one another with nimble fingers, each taking time
to lick herbs and spices off the other in a hundred
strokes from tongues that name the basil, thyme,
pepper and pimento in that single, unmade bed:
each licking the plate of the other so clean,
there's no need to wash those plates again.

For freedom, read desire. Once he is fixed,
the second he jumps up, she shows him the door.
She doesn't want to be the one who's ditched
first, not in her own home. He looks floored,
but she takes that as his surprise that she pipped
him to the post. Does this make her a whore?
A woman has to do very little in a man's eyes,
to cross the line from venerated to despised.

But this man is different. He refuses to go.
He tells her how he really feels about
her, things he never felt for himself, 'muchless no
one.' She will have to kill him to drive him out.
They square off like this, neither willing to
give in. Minutes pass. Flies circle both.
She is rigid; he trembles; static bits off each
travel between them conducted by heat.

As she begins to tremble, he grows calm.
Her eyes moisten, his become less wet.
Suddenly, she raises and spreads her arms.
He falls forward into her with hardly a step.
They squeeze, rock and wail like alarms,
and promise everlasting companionship:
Tom, I love you more than I love myself.
Stella, I will love you to my last breath.

You know the rest: how she trains him
to ferry runaways to the next safe residence,
sleeping days, working nights, singing hymns
to God's glory for designing their alliance;
up to the point where he poses as tree-limbs
and bark in the dark in a shadow-dance –
I mean the disco-flicker of those lamps
and those hunting men's retro-chants.

Thanks to her, Tom's romance with that tree
finishes happily. The men leave him stranded.
One hand cups his genitals. His nudity
adds to his confusion. Though he commands
a good sense of direction, the hand that's free
feels out tree and dark, water and land.
When he stops with his arm up like a shoot,
he looks as if he's put down roots.

Then he spots lamplight and hears his name
in a familiar tone, more like a deep drawl.
Is he hallucinating? Should he remain
incognito? When the light grows small
and the voice withdraws, Tom knows that strain
can only belong to one woman. He calls
scrambling towards the shining speck,
Stella! It's Tom! Stella! Come back!

Did he wait too long? Quiet returns
once his shout dies down as if Stella
were among the heavens, a hole burned
into the outsized circus tent of the constella-
tions, a remote pulse ringed like Saturn.
Her face outlined by shifting stars tells a
different story; his heaven-sent chords
perpetually returning stripped of his words.

How long Tom does stand, frozen, ears peeled,
eyes drinking darkness, soaking it up like mops
aimed at a thick oil-slick, as if night had spilled
into day and soldered everything, his mouth-drop
held as if a slack jaw can listen and breathe,
replacing ears and lungs, or make time stop?
How long is a piece of string? An eternity
if, like Tom, you're stuck with a slave's reality.

What happens next Tom wouldn't condone,
an act many suppose undignified
in a grown man, especially an old one,
but when you have nothing to lose, pride
is the least of your worries: Tom drops on
his knees and sobs in his hands like a child,
a toy wound up by the key of his grief
and set loose trembling towards relief.

His head could take a lifetime of servitude
since it didn't involve his heart, but one miss
of love's beat threatens to break him in two,
reduce him to rubble, a wreck, dismiss
all wisdom banked from verisimilitude,
incrementally, from stick and whip in this
long life where laughter and joy are rare gifts
leaving a sour look that won't shift.

Tom! Too busy crying to begin to hear.
Again, Tom! His ears fill but he doesn't stop.
Tom! Too far from his name to begin to care.
Tom! His right hand shields his face, his left cups
his genitals, both stung by his name in the air.
His promise of freedom to that young couple up
in smoke, with them drowned or, worse
captured, 'What a loving God!' he cursed.

'Tom!' This time admonishing and familiar.
'Stella? Stella! You came. For me? Me?'
She throws her shawl over his sloped shoulder,
'Yes, Tom. For you. Don't look too happy.'
Her arm holds the shawl still, and him.
She takes his hand and they leave those trees.
'I lost a young couple to that river,
Stella, or else they're in the hands of connivers.

'They trusted me and I let them slip
out of my hand.' Tom, sobbing, continued
his rant and rave, Stella touched his lips,
immediately he stalled and quietened.
They shuffled along. Cicadas leapt
from the path, silencing their disquietude,
resuming – only after the two passed –
with pique and contempt, plainly unimpressed.

Tom cried himself to sleep in Stella's bed.
'I should have drowned in that river or got caught.
I've had my life. They're too young to be
in such trouble. And so in love. They should not
trust old men who're only good for counting beads;
old men with dry hearts and big mouths.'
All Stella could say was no to everything
and hold him, rock him and shush him.

Stella remembered the moment she died
as a woman and person and the shell
of the rest of her days took over her insides.
She was nine or ten, she wasn't sure, you couldn't tell,
carrying a message for her master with pride
but with a child's bearing and on a child's stroll.
At the crossroads she saw a man in a cage
hoisted from a tree, barely a man's age;

a battalion of flies; a mass of bones and flesh;
a gauze woven an acre wide of the particular
stench of clotted blood, and that blood in a nest
at the foot of the cage, drop by peculiar
drop falling in strings, adding to the mess
underneath, each string breaking to form another.
She screamed, turned and ran, not glancing back,
feeling that cage gaining on her back.

Her sweat became that blood, the man's skin
her skin. She fought for each shallow breath.
Somehow she'd caught the dead man's stink.
She swallowed air but tasted blood and death.
She scrubbed herself; refused food and drink.
When questioned she tried but couldn't speak.
Rescued from scrubbing, she only ate
soap and went four days straight awake.

They pinned her and forced food down,
mixed with bush tea doubling as sleep medicine,
boiled by them into a deep-green alluvium,
burying any leftovers of that nameless, certain
plant, coveted and antediluvian,
spoken about in hushed tones, unwritten.
It made her sleep but her eyes refused to close;
still seeing the cage with that man in no clothes.

She's no longer a girl or an African.
She died on her feet, propelled by rage.
She fled her body as only the free can.
Asleep, she replaces him in his cage
at the crossroads. Her body's all broken,
an oil-slick of her blood mirrors her visage,
there for all to see what becomes of the slave
who tries to rise above the station of the trade.

Stella knew a part of Tom died among
those trees by that river. Covered in earth,
more mud than man, he lost his tongue.
Rough on top but smooth underneath,
she craved its love, its peculiar pabulum:
wet, muscled, hungry with hot breath.
Now tongueless, an unstrung instrument,
Tom shook from head to toe in silence.

She would not let any more of him die.
There are many deaths in a slave's life,
and for each death a little peace flies
away from the sum of trouble and strife
that is a slave's lot, that a slave must abide
until a stone or shell is all that's left.
She could not go back to living alone,
she'd kill herself than be a shell or stone.

For every step he took from her she made
two towards him. She talked the whole
time, talking him back to her, afraid
that words as a bond, a lifeline, a goal,
a bank, or grafted skin between two frail,
but independent bodies would not hold.
She held him so close they hardly seemed
to breathe apart. Her gaze held his, her twin beams

captured his faint look. Their bodies were
indistinguishable one from the next.
She watched him like a newborn to reassure
herself that the fluttering soul, vexed
to awake in such a quivering body, never-
theless stayed, that it would remain fixed
to that flesh, would not quit its toe-
hold on life. For if it ceased hers would too.

So they spent the nights and days, or those
days and nights spent them. Her eyes wide,
his narrow. He lying on his belly, nose
buried in a pillow, she on her back beside
him with the crook of her arm transposed
into a pillow under her head, one hand astride
his back, stroking it, coaxing him away from
agitation towards peace, or its notion.

Two bodies, enmeshed, intertwined,
with two thinking hearts in unison,
or two numbed, interconnected minds,
that's really one mind in two locations,
their breathing synchronized, twinned,
a pairs event for swimmers whose gyrations
win gold; di-zygotic twins, living in anticipation
of each other's next thought and action.

She smiles, checks herself, bites her lips,
releases Tom, slithers from the warm bed
to the corner, designated her kitchen, tip-
toes there, grabs the sharpest, biggest blade
she can find by touch in the half-dark, half-lit
room, raises that knife in both hands held
high in her tightest grip, and with rigid steps,
her joints stiff, her body covered in sweat,

she walks zombie-fashion towards Tom.
The blade is so clean it catches the meagre
morning light unawares, gathers it into
a knife's shape and flicks it as several eager
knives, soundlessly, about the room.
Tom's strapped to the bed and that gyre
for a bed spins and she is the blindfolded
knife-thrower who aims to miss that bed.

She stops and towers above Tom with her
arms raised fully. She brings them down
hard into the back of Tom, between his shoulder
blades. Air fizzes from a punctured lung,
his limbs thrash and go limp, blood fires
around the room replacing the stung
light with a dark red. Stella screams,
and bolts upright from her bad dream.

Now Tom comforts her, as she explains
her nightmare. He tells her how lucky
she is that the worse things in her life are imagined
not real. He is upbeat, honest, even plucky.
He says he knows she'll never harm him,
and, a lie, that he hasn't slept more soundly
in his life. Now he holds her, lying face up,
she on her side nestled into him; saucer and cup.

They lose track of their thoughts. They snooze.
They wake up laughing. Light builds around
their laughter. Night thins to an elastic ooze,
a tactile translucency, no sound.
Delicate as a web, overnight dew bruises
then breaks, but not before diamonds
bubble so that first light makes
a tiara adding to it until it disintegrates.

Who said Tom and Stella were past their prime?
Ya, ya, yippee, yippee, ya, ya, yeah.
They know to make hay while the sun shines.
Ya, ya, yippee, yippee, ya, ya, yeah.
Love and desire always looking for good times.
Ya, ya, yippee, yippee, ya, ya, yeah.
Young and old are flesh and blood, skin and bone.
Tom and Stella too wise to leave love and lust alone.

Tom and Stella can teach us all something.
Something, ting-a-ling, something, ting-a-ling.
How to grow old and keep love's sting.
Sting, ting-a-ling, sting, ting-a-ling.
Love in the eyes, love under the skin.
The skin, ting-a-ling, the skin, ting-a-ling.
They going to the grave, ting-a-ling,
to the grave, not fighting, ting-a-ling, but loving.

War

Tom and Stella saw an army widen the road
with their northward march led by a flag
with too few stars and too many bars that they would
live under if that army won. Its progress dragged
Africans and history on a march backwards,
eyes in front, arms swinging, as if blacks had
the gift of sight in the back of their heads,
or history's forward march were dead.

Black men swelled the ranks of two armies.
North met South and a geography bled,
a dye that ran from banks of men, too many
to count, men the colour of ochre and lead,
from the hibiscus, iron ore, magne-
sium and bauxite of earth turned, seeded
with fallen men, ploughed by wild ox
and not enough wood for each to have a box.

Ash rained for days, months, years.
Sun magnified the glint of swords.
Flint and powder flung thunder and spears
of lightning in fields, valleys and woods.
Flesh tore, bones and teeth splintered
with a noise of flour sacks (triple sewed)
ripped open, or paddy bags, or the dry
husk torn off coconuts with a hoarse cry.

Bayonets opened men's heads like oysters.
Men's hearts sealed like clams netted too early.
Their words became guns drawn from holsters.
Their tongues forked and atrophied,
cut out with their hearts, ears, fingers, livers,
genitals and eyes, all taken for trophies.
Each star in the flag darkened to a hole
punctured in a girl's new camisole.

Bush and flower yielded to the widening road.
Trees bowed or uprooted with trespass.
Fields fell fallow or bloomed blood, grow-
ing acres of uniformed bones. Canvas
replaced skin, replaced flesh. Men rode
horses over fields of razor grass;
but every blade was a human skull,
and every skull was a hurt done to that girl.

There were no longer men, nor animals,
nor anything but opposing flags,
borders drawn by trees, rivers, terminal
mountain ranges and the weather dragged
across them. Sun and moon kept journals,
building a library of dead name-tags.
The light fed the ground, spineless light;
the men fed the light, bones that were bright.

Tom and Stella sheltered deep in forests.
They crouched past armies. They resembled mud
mixed with pounded leaves and became the driest
of cracked barks, eating worms and slugs,
sleeping upright, back to back, in snatches.
Awake, they held each other's gaze and hugged,
afraid to look anywhere in case they saw
another field littered with the life that was.

Tom and Stella trained their ears to each
other's names and nothing else, no cries
of the dying, no chants of the killing, no speech
recruiting more men, no mules or horses
neighing, braying, kicking as the life seeped
from them. They heard a language of sighs
from wind in the trees, rain on leaves and sticks,
a hoof on mud and stone, a mandible click.

Tom and Stella abutting battlefields skirted
men tearing each other apart; how
sometimes a single blow to the head shirked
off by one man can lay another low;
how the man lying there looks unhurt,
not dead; while it takes twenty cuts to throw
the hard-headed one and twenty more
to bring him, human-strange, to death's door.

Death disconnects the wires in his skull.
Death drowns the flame in his thighs.
Death crumbles the rice paper of his lungs.
Death hollows the brittle bulbs of his eyes.
Death curls his fingers, furs his tongue.
Death irons out the crease of his smile.
Death piles him on a mountain of stiffs,
and welcomes more disciples of still life.

Tom and Stella corked their ears against
soldier after soldier crying for death to hurry
and finish what it had begun, their mechanist
training to kill or be killed suddenly
failing them, unable to stomach the loneliness
of lying in a battlefield helpless to do any-
thing for themselves and feeling a body, theirs,
disintegrate to leave the shell of a soldier.

Death empties their heads of all they'd thought
and done up to that moment. They cannot take
their beloved memories being erased. They cry out
for death to stop playing with them and strike;
strike them down or let them live to return south
or north and surrender their guns for a rake,
saw and plough, and their arms full of a lover
again, heads emptied of hate no soil can cover.

Tom and Stella can't help listening. Their pores
soak up men becoming manure, a puzzle
of broken bones, a name and date on scores
of graves, an absence in a partner's bed, a ghazal
sung by wife or child, past tense in the discourse
of the living. With every pore an ear, they guzzle
up history even as history brushes them off
as an old man and woman who have had enough.

Burnt flesh thickened the air, skin alive
with worms darkened in the sun and moon,
suspending seasons, building a worm-hive,
adding its own abundant, stink-perfume
to everything. Not the world we live
in and know, but the world we don't presume
to know, propels us towards death;
a world flesh and bone can't defeat.

Men marched from one known fighting place
to another, alert to the strangeness in-between:
what can't be touched, smelled, heard, tasted
or talked about, if by a miracle it is seen;
what, Stella says, can only be intimated
in an involuntary shudder, or dream
that recurs; what most people call God
and His design for want of a better word.

Men fired at reflections and echoes.
Rode horses into fog and over cliffs.
Lay down with a saddle for a pillow
and the elements for a whore or wife.
Smiled that special smile reserved for a foe
who cannot be defeated; not in this life.
These men who proclaim a reverence
for all living things, offer this defence:

that the good crop must be kept separate
from the bad, otherwise the good rots as well;
that should a caged bird die trying to escape,
that bird is better off than settling for a cell;
that life means nothing in an unfree state,
to free it, men must die and men must kill.
An army for a locked-up bird, a single crop,
a fledgling state; an enemy as unwanted rot.

How then would it ever come to an end?
Birds abandoned their nests, eggs rotted
or bald young with their mouths opened
and necks craned, fell back dead,
or forward, from ornate nests to the land.
Moles, beavers, raccoons scrambled ahead
of the armies, or found themselves trapped
by the two. The continent cleared except

for soldiers. The sky seemed to retreat
to a safer distance. Sun and moon became
remote objects facing away from the earth,
dodging behind cloud, reluctant, ashamed
to provide light for a theatre of death,
light for men to see to hate and maim:
neither the light of life nor the light of love
reinvigorated humanity from above.

Tom and Stella wished they had wings
or were blind, enough to burrow past
front lines, though they were wearing
the dye of trees, mud, stone and grass.
They prayed for rain, torrential, howling,
to start and not stop until it could wash
off encampments, float cannon and sword-hilt
downstream, block and blunt them with silt.

Let rain lift men from dugouts, from saddles,
from lines drawn on maps, and put them down
miles apart. Let it cleanse their souls!
So they prayed on their knees, not for their own,
but the salvation of others, prayed the whole
night into an eerily unsung, worm-free dawn;
held their faces to glass and drank their images;
gathered swollen mushrooms and chewed sage.

Tom says he was never young enough
to die for a cause and now that he has one,
he's too old to fight. His body, broken though
it is, would take the place of these young
people, than be left behind to pick through
a battlefield and bury another man's son.
Men splinter, rip, and crumble apart;
china skulls, muslin skin and bones of earth.

Bodies are webs strung across a door,
egg-shell bodies, cloud for flesh, smoke
for breath, overnight, ashen frost for
skin; valley-mist bodies stroked
to death by the first light that pours
onto them; feather bodies that float
without breaking a pond's dusty skin;
that think they are rocks, thunder and lightning.

Here comes a man, not a fucking mountain.
He steps and blood clears from his feet
under his weight and rushes back again
when he raises his foot for the next step.
His bones shuffle, clack and crack in the basin,
bucket and sack of his body. He forgets
he bears the water of how and who he is
from the well and womb out of which he rises.

He grins and bears it until he loses or drops
the responsibility. He spills and spreads,
thinning out when he dies. All his skip, hop,
and fetch-it years, his carrying of himself, heads
towards this sudden surrender, this collapse
of his carefully stacked bones, the webs
of veins and spirit-level balanced blood;
a life of memories coming to a flood.

And all the time he carried himself like stone.
He bumped into things expecting them
to move. He stood in the open all alone
in lightning. At midday, he lay in the sun, then
stared at it and stared at it until it shone
from the exits of his body, all ten.
He became an inspiration to himself;
his skin peeled, he went blind and deaf.

A bullet, a sword, a long march aimed
at a mountain range and gorgeous valley,
could be absorbed, so these young flames,
in the guise of the impregnable, simply
believed. They sang, devoured wild game,
grumbled over the lack of an enemy,
in sight, saw this chance to fight and kill
as a welcomed break from farms and mills.

The mother hates how her country consumes
her days, yet spares her, savouring the morsel
of her son. Her country always presumes
too much about her, yet keeps counsel
elsewhere, refusing to enter rooms
she occupies. Her mothering parcels
her son for war when all she means to do
is love him the way she was taught to.

He walks away with hugs, kisses and a wave,
straight into the arms of a war that squeezes
his body into an early, mass grave,
and punishes everyone his chivalry leaves
behind with thoughts of how they failed to save
him from himself. Bees and breeze
scatter his spores. He becomes a field
of peach grass, a lily, gifts of the wild.

Peace

Stella and Tom dream a new rust-
ic country, spun from an orange sun
and moon bright as elephant tusks,
and clay from a river so malleable one
can plait it; and goat skin with the must-
y stink still in it but elastic as moonlight on
water; a land where the animals kill
to eat rather than eat to kill.

In their land people run around unclothed.
They make song using the single blade
of razor grass and poetry from what we throw
away: hair, banana peel, a broken clay
pot, perspiration. It's a land at the rainbow's
end; a dream they always wake from afraid.
The main ingredient of what they conjure
is that the races love one another.

In this dream nobody suffers for their race.
There is no lasting north–south split.
Stella knows Tom explores this place
when she holds him and his body sticks
to hers with heat and sweat and his face
glows. Tom knows Stella's trick:
she complains that he's too fiery to hold
to escape the dream, but she doesn't let go.

Stella, always soft in his arms, and hot,
feels good to Tom with his tongue on her pale
inner elbow, or in the sunken, silky spot
as he calls it, of her sex. If that tale
were a real country rebuilt from top
to bottom, and a person, then Stella
would be it, a cartographer's dream-trip
charting her body with fingers and lips.

And then there are all the hidden places
of her heart that he will spend all his days
discovering, and all the untold spaces
he will never get to know that blind his gaze
when she casts him those upward glances
of hers, showing the lower whites of her eyes,
the deep trawl of her considered speech,
her wading-water-way of crossing a street.

Sometimes she'll lay a hand on him and when
she removes it he'll ache for more of her touch,
burning for her, his eyes following her as a wren,
no, bat, tracks a moth. She busies herself at such
times to increase his hunger, swinging her gen-
erous hips with one arm thrown out to catch
her balance and a basin wedged above her hip
with some useful thing (or not) in it –

the peas to shell or the shells of peas –
bending at the waist to tidy a patch of floor,
deliberately, without having bent her knees,
so that her dress rides up her legs, and for
the sweetness of feeling his eyes freeze
on her, holding that lean, showing more
thigh than anything. But it's what he can't
see that gives Tom the jitters like he has ants.

Then she passes close enough to brush
him with her dress. Her scent is a cool,
definite atmosphere, a sudden rush
of air, dragging desire in her wake. Too
close and he grabs that arm, the brash
right arm, held out and swinging, and pulls
her and clasps his arms around her back
to bar her flight; her hard body goes slack.

She laughs, a soft chuckle, reserved for
times she believed would never arise;
warmer for him than he could ever
be for her, she guesses. But look inside
his head and she'd see the same desire
criss-crossing his mind: that he's alive
not dead, that he should pinch himself to prove
a slave's life could end in peace and love.

Their shared dream – also a fantasy
since they entertain it awake and asleep –
brings Africa back as geography
from the clouded heart and head, the deep
space, without borders, of ancestry,
to cliffs and coasts before they sweep
inland to villages, fields, herds,
water from a well too sweet for words.

Africa makes Tom hungry a lot:
bush-meat in a groundnut stew, pounded
yams, and red peppers in a pepper-pot,
always this well-water to wash it down,
calming the mind, soothing the lips and mouth.
He eats and still feels hungry as a hound,
a need Mother Africa alone satisfies,
as if Africa were a meal not a fantasy.

He presses his fists into his belly to quell
the feeling, but Africa does not lessen.
The more he kneads his midriff, the greater
his need of Africa. While he hoped
to smother the place like a landfill,
he massaged life into it; he provoked
it till his body ached for a residency
it had to have; a vitamin deficiency.

There has to be a place for him in Africa
since there is space for Africa in him.
He feels a hole open inside after
an urge to stuff his mouth with mud; the whim
surfaces, grips and sticks, as paprika
in meals returns in sweat and stains on skin.
Chewing a piece of bark quells it somehow,
don't ask me how, I've no proof to show.

It all involves the spine, the sap of trees,
and history. All three in a preservation
conspiracy with a people's need to be free;
a threatened species' need for conservation;
with a little bit of you and a little bit of me
thrown in, and all the scientific observation
in the world couldn't account for it;
nor God, nor any number of edicts.

Instead, tune in to cows jumping the moon –
cows moo(n)ing as they jump – and you touch
the right track. Go primitive, and soon
(as it did for Josephine Baker) it makes much
more sense. Take it from me, I have lived through
all three or had them live through me: a munch
or bite of tree-sap is worse than its bark;
history is shelves of human spines in the dark.

Soon the hole takes over Tom's skull.
He sees himself in a country the opposite
of everything he knows: a sun that's dull,
a moon in place of a sun it's so bright,
a crescent sun, a never-ending circle
for a moon, with the sea in the sky
and the sun blossoming in a sea of sand;
night-time closes them all in its hands.

A topsy-turvy land with all the parts of all
the animals he knows or hears about
shuffled around to make African animals.
With the roots of trees above ground, flout-
ing the hug of earth, and branches stalled
below, and ships sailing clean throughout
African air among grazing whale-deer;
when they stampede it's quake-thunder.

Africa booms in his head, makes him rock
on his feet, forward to the tips of his toes,
and back onto his heels. He is African stock!
Africa races in his chest and when it slows
he has to feel for his heart, listen and clock
the signs that Africa has not closed
down, that it lives in him still; he checks
for Africa in his wrist, chest, groin and neck.

What colour is an African sea? Not gray,
nor green nor sky. Not the sea that brought
Africans here, with its traitorous salt-spray.
Something not seen before, a sea wrought
from a planet other than earth – a hay
colour, yellow, lemon, saffron, yet tough.
And the water keeps permanent tracks
so that it is possible to retrace steps back.

What floats in this sea? Not only ships.
This African sea is not hungry for flesh.
It keeps everything buoyant on its
surface. It stains all sea-worthy vessels
bright yellow from bulkhead to bow-sprit.
One would have to think twice to unleash
an anchor since it bounces on this jello
sea and must hook onto skin that's yellow.

An African sea-bed is not littered with bones
but a bright alphabet of scattered and jumbled
letters in yellow seaweed and yellow sponges,
too porous to read when reassembled,
yellowed by sea, erased by time and honed
in current, turning for fish until it crumbles
into yellow sand, adding to the hieroglyphics
of coral a new maths, biology and physics.

Stella likes Tom's Africa but says too much
happens there. Hers is a small plot
by comparison: a house made of mud, a hutch,
hidden from sight, far from other huts,
surrounded by trees and vines that catch
ankles and choke vegetation; a spot
so private sunlight never sets the scene;
the light it grows is always shaded green.

Her sea has to be a long way off, its salt
barely discernible in any breeze.
She can follow her whims in her cobalt
Africa, and often they will leave
her weak and trembling after their assault,
or else they dictate that, were she to sneeze
today, she'd upset the patterned light
falling slanted through trees in sound-bites.

Stella dances there and laughs unguarded.
The fruits on trees are no longer bitter.
She does not have to steal from her own yard
fruits once left on limbs to rot rather
than given to slaves who were half-starved.
She pickles them, puts them into pepper-
pot stews, dries them for the off-season,
makes jam and brews sundry teas with some.

She's hidden her hair under a scarf for years.
In her Africa, heads are braided and dyed ochre,
and beaded in old and young, and left bare,
open, with faces, arms, neck, shoulders.
And sometimes only a calico wrap near
the waist, leaving the chest uncovered.
Eyes look as eyes must and maybe tongues
wag as they tend to when people mill around.

Stella is a woman again in her Africa.
She keeps her children and names them
all what she wants them to be in America:
Happiness, Prosperity, Freedom.
Grandmother Stella, a miracle-
worker in a floor-length dress whose hem
drags on the floorboards of her log cabin
as she mixes her remedies and sings.

More a hum than a song. There are folks
who will survive Stella and bear her name. Trees
older than Slavery surround her. Oaks
planted by her before her children breathed
shade saplings put down to welcome a fourth
generation destined to walk the earth free;
taller, straighter, stronger than those shoots,
that will overtake them and branch out.

And if Africa means she does not know Tom?
Then she will do without it and accept what
Slavery throws at her to have him in her home.
Slavery has taken most things but not
everything. Her ability to sing isn't gone.
Just this morning her windpipe worked up
a tune. She saw her and him cut to shreds
by their first embrace, yet neither bled.

She wonders when she stopped being African
in this land. Born here to a mother whose
mother came from Africa, were not regions
of her, however remote, fashioned after those
strange parts? Slavery in this new land
shaped her. In old age she would choose
to be African rather than the nothing
that a slave is. Africa is something.

Africa in America. Catch a goat.
Take a sharp blade, rub it against stone.
Brace the goat and yourself and cut its throat.
Drain the blood into calabash, ignore the moan
of ropy liquid against the gourd; throw
sand on the spot to prevent dogs homing
in on that coagulating blood. Skin the carcass.
Stretch the skin over wood for one purpose.

It stinks and dries in an indirect sun.
The meat is ready for a pot, dying to be cured,
parcelled out to family and friends, the horns
ground into powder then mixed into a puree
with herbs, the feet for a broth (the scrotum
is a delicacy), the tongue peppered
for stew, the tail continues to whisk flies,
the hooves walk mountainous clouds in the sky.

Skin over wood. Hollow wood.
Stretched skin. Hands talk to heart.
Boneless hands. Thinking heart. A flood
of understanding comes to that part
of the wood beneath that skin about the good
imbued by hands coming down smart
on it, fluid fingers flowing above the skin,
flattering it with touch-talk, and it sings.

A continent in sound. Sound brings
a continent across the sky and sea.
A continent shaped by hands on skin
sacrificed by a goat who must have seen
his soul fluting, not on a heady mountain
ledge, but airborne, dragging this parachute free
of its moorings, relocating an archipelago
in sounds of souls no longer cargo.

Until goat talked it down to the ground,
coaxed it up through the soles of our feet
into our chest and our head and our tongue.
It is a lost, forgotten place, missing teeth
worried by our tongue, something we long
for, dream of, but won't know if we meet.
The Africa we never got to know,
sprung in the America we reap and sow.

Our heads spin with this posited place.
Our skulls resonate with our captured past.
It weighs our hearts, brimming all the spaces
between with all the things we feel we've lost.
Our flesh aches and only pains less when faced
with drum talk; drum bringing down the ghost
of Africa from dreams, down through history,
and up up up through flesh and blood stories.

When Tom first hears about Africa
he thinks slaves have circumvented their hurt
with their version of a heaven freer
than paradise because right here on earth,
until he listens to the drum concertina,
a continent into two hands, two hands worth
a continent; and if those hands are driven
by a body and soul then their art is heaven.

But the sea, the unassailable sea,
where Time drowned and Africa floated,
both lost to slaves, both in water's company,
leaves Tom feeling there's a fishbone in his throat,
that Africa had never been, would never be
more than something stirred by the goat-
skin drum, a waking dream that lasts
only as long as the song of the drum blasts.

He fancies every flock heading for a trap,
their chevrons marking a winding road in air
erased by the sea, a road not on any map,
except that each heartbeat sends a chevron flair
radiating through his body, sketching this gap:
his head that is Africa tapers into a cadaver
that's the sea; the rise and fall of his body,
a current in his veins; his neck is an estuary.

If he listens to the drum with flesh and bone,
and his African head, he finds his way back
to Africa through movement and tone.
The time he lost is measured out on the track
of his spine that buckles, curves, snaps, hones
itself to time and Africa and the ship's deck
of the sea, now over him, shuffling its boards,
now under him, like a spine without a cord.

The sea holds still long enough for him to draw
a map. Air stirs without disturbing the markers
arranged by a migratory flock. Clouds crawl
across the tinged canvas stretched over-
head, a cartographer's dream, all raw
in unbounded love of gradients and contours.
Night lights up the compass points that Tom
navigates by; the drum is his metronome.

His body twitches in recognition of the rhythm
of ship on sea and wind in sails; no land
in sight; not a hint of vegetation in the hymn
of that wind, nor in the reflection of sky and
sea in each other's mirror held up for him
in a choreography Tom understands
fully but every time deliberately forgets,
just to experience more deeply the next.

Stella lifts her dress above her knees
to free her legs for little kicks, stamps
and flicks of heel, instep and balls of feet.
She shakes bits of Africa from the damp
American soil that when dry frees
so much dust an African edifice jams
against the sky and Stella climbs its ladder
back through time to her ancestors.

Tom walks in his Africa with a stick
his height, cut from a polished balsam
that weighs so little, if he were to stick
his long, straightened, weaker right arm
out in front or to the side and keep a grip
on that superstitious, lucky charm,
he would not have to think nor strain
to hold it there: that pole *is* Tom's aim.

It nudges cattle along a narrow track.
It rests Tom's upper body when he's at work,
standing with his bad foot jammed back
on the knee of the left leg. He's like a stork
while he leans on that rod. You catch
sight of the two and see one body, not a stalk
and a man; you marvel at the extent of it;
wondering how on earth he manages that trick.

Stella keeps calabashes in all guises
and sizes, to pick rice clean of husks,
dip water from a barrel, store surprises,
cool tea. For this she knows she must
hold a tune and a steady hand. She uses
two gourds. It's one of her daily tasks.
She separates her hands as she pours
to allow a long flow between gourds.

She gets as much air as possible on the tea
without spilling any. Her hands come back
together in plenty of time to completely
empty one gourd and begin pouring black
tea from the other. She hums a field ditty.
Something about the long hours and lack
of sleep, reward and a proper diet;
the staple design to keep slaves quiet.

Tom takes his cup with honey. Stella drinks
hers straight. It's the tea of penury.
The tea of repentance. The tea of thanks
for surviving the nightmares to see
dawn, well, yes, dawn. For a time that stinks,
a time to forget, regret, this is the tea.
Drink it and maybe all your troubles
brewed and stewed in one cup can be gobbled.

She wakes with a dry mouth and sleepy
from her fitful slumber. That cup at that time –
for all its historical baggage – is the remedy.
The heat, the wet, the caffeine, the taste, combine
(no, stronger) conspire, each day to ready
her to face a life she's more inclined
to skip, if she had the choice: suicide
is no option, life is for living, she decides.

Tom props his friend and walking companion
outside the front door as if for defence.
He ducks into the hut's kept Cimmerian
dark and cosseted cool with a step-dance
over the door mound that holds back rain,
insects and spirits, ducking and prancing
at the same time. His body curls a little
and shrinks defensively crossing that doorsill.

What if a bad spirit is there lying in wait
for him, sent by a man meaning him harm?
Or enough insects to bear an adult's weight?
Or one with a sting that can fell an army?
People see that stick and realise he is at
home; if it's laid flat they know better than
to bother him; on the odd occasion
he raises it if someone is too brazen.

Stella stacks her calabashes at right-
angles against walls and trees to drain
dry and smell of brittle sunlight.
At dusk she picks up the biggest basin
first and loads the smaller ones inside.
She reaches the last and smallest contain-
er and, because she has named every one,
ushers it up with a high-pitched sermon.

She could be coaxing, cajoling chicks to eat
the leftovers she sows in her acreage,
for them to gather and peck around her feet.
This is Stella with her phantom lineage;
the flesh and blood she dreams she'll meet.
Only her calabashes can enter her cottage
and (minus what she calls *that stick*) Tom,
looking naked without his totem.

He sees himself using *that stick*, as Stella
dubs it, to clear a path, strewn with fragments
of calabash, to the front door; his medulla
oblongata-like mind likened to the contents
of said calabash before now by her: all
gray mush, mulch and no essence.
He fears the end calabash come to: sliced
in two, scraped out, their half-shells dried.

Would a sane person actually choose
to be a slave? Tom's unequivocal
answer is yes, if it means being those
empty halves of calabash. Why so vocal
on the subject, Tom? Is it because
calabash have no features, are unequal,
divided and gutted? Slaves scheme
to be free. Calabash do not dream.

A head if struck opens as loud, grained
and messy as calabash. Tom should know.
Before you try to part that knot in his brain,
ply him with rum, pussyfoot rather than elbow
your way around or risk him bursting a vein
in his temple should he start to curse and throw
his weight around, driving you from him
with a tongue the devil envies more than sin.

If Tom decides to talk he'll say he upped
and walked, without looking back, from a furrow
he grew old in, to liberty. Don't interrupt,
fidget, fart, look away, yawn, or show
any signs of boredom or he will stop.
Wait for the juicy part about how
only one final obstacle stood
between him and his freedom for good.

If you wait and he gets that far you'll hear
why he hates the idea of calabash.
That final hurdle was an overseer.
Tom's single possession was a cutlass.
Need I go on? The man's head was bare,
tired and bored. The sun was sinking fast.
He pinned his eye onto a shiny object
encased in mud which he kneeled to inspect.

Tom jumped at this chance: he brought
the blade down on the skull so swift and hard
he broke the bone and sliced clean through,
dividing that head into unequal halves
sounding, looking, smelling and with the rough
texture of calabash. While the slaves
scattered, Tom walked his famous walk,
and entered the history of folk-talk.

As years accrue he climbs higher branches
just to procure the same quality stick.
Lower branches are stripped by goats, vines,
cows and mischief-ridden children who lick
the leaves of trees for the salt that lines
their weathered fronts and the light flicked
off their undersides. Curse them. Bless them.
They act blindly, without malice or strategem.

Stella concedes that calabash cannot think,
though their limbs grow like thoughts
in multiple directions, double and slink
back on themselves, run over stone like broth
over dumplings and climb a tree's trunk.
Calabash have more use than most mort-
als in Stella's eyes. She paints and decorates
them with stick figures wrapped in ochres.

She wishes the articulate vines
said something illuminating about
her condition, as calabash at times
emulated her situation in the South,
keeping their shape, smoothness and shine
in adversity, surrendering without
losing dignity. Losing life, losing face
while retaining vestiges of grace.

Stella and Tom in their old age cross
their hearts and knock on wood in gratitude
that war entrenched for years finally passes.
Between her calabash and his stick, lassitude
reigns. They doze like cats. Graze like horses.
Scratch their backs on doorframes. Their attitude
to everything is, if it is so urgent
it will happen without their attention.

They are right and they are wrong. The world
carries on as it must, but it is diminished
without their involvement. America unfurls
a new flag and makes amends with the vanquished.
For a while Tom and Stella ride this crest of equal
opportunity barely started before it finishes.
The South is the closest they come to Africa;
Carolina's hills, a mule and forty acres.

They trade what they grow for the few things
tended ground cannot fashion: pots and pans,
knives and horse-shoes, and a little flint
to light a stove then a clay pipe, not Tom's
but Stella's. She creases her face to squint
through the smoke signals her lips form
with popping sounds punctuating grand plans
she never completes, instead she abandons.

Stella's smoke waters Tom's eyes.
He talks about the two he could not save:
Faith and Christy tip the scales against the lives
of all the folks combined who he conveyed
successfully to liberty. Though he tries
not to let it, that scale with those two weighs
heavy on his heart. He finds himself stuck
in the middle of doing something he forgot.

Or else he walks and can't remember why
he set out or what he wanted to do.
Stella's smoke cannot be seen yet his eyes
stream. He meanders back to her with a stew-
teeth (air sucked in that makes a high-
pitched sound) as if his proximity to
her regains his bearings and equilibrium.
Smoke wets his face; lightens the opprobrium

in his heart and head over Christy and Faith.
Stella locks eyes with Tom and both hearts skip
a beat brimming with so much love so late
in life. She says nothing of her failed trips,
losses she took years to accept as the state
of things, like that basin wedged to her hip
(minus any value) she walks the yard with
daily; balancing her, balancing it;

precious as the particularly strafing light
Tom sees her in, that stirs his blood from thick
to thin, from warm to hot, despite his ripe
old age. She passes and he grabs her quick.
She moans there's work to do. They horse-fight.
She puts her basin next to his walking stick.
They step briskly indoors, arms entwined;
their lips, belly and hips become joined.

Tom swings in a hammock he can't climb out of
unaided. Stella steadies it for him.
His legs drop over the side followed by, 'Okay, love,'
then his bony body. He looks as if he left his skin
behind in that crinkled hammock like a hand a glove,
or the feeling an amputee keeps for a limb.
When he's in that hammock, it's him all over;
that canvas suits him like skin or his lover.

Stella's turn. He steadies it for her. 'Thanks, Tom.'
She spreads the fabric and sits with a creak
from the main beam her hammock hangs from
that, once she settles, sounds about to break
and bring the roof down, but it's a metronome
for each swing or speech if a house could speak:
telling all the things it sees from up above;
all the, 'Take my hand's. Thanks Tom's. 'Okay, love's;

the this and that of touch, gesture and look;
the so-so's, the such-and-such of those two;
their one step, two step, twist, line and hook
for each other; their wordless knowing what to do,
when and how, in their to-and-fro, ebb-and-flow book
of days from which I take a page for me, for you,
for Faith, Christy, and every couple since,
and for the new century I have to convince.

Mrs Mason

The war over, Christy finds himself beside
Faith's grave. Mr Mason has fled
to one of the Leeward Islands to reside,
sans Mrs Mason, and I am presumed dead,
missing at sea. Christy's too tired
to cry. A mental tsunami wrecks his head.
He drops to his knees to improvise a prayer,
more a curse against Slavery, his love's slayer.

He castigates himself for planting the seed
that cost Faith her life and blasts me too
for failing her. But Mrs Mason told him he'd
done what most men would never do,
what would not cross their minds, muchless get said:
by coming this far for a slave he had proved true
to his word. But Christy's violent retort
which he blurted out, cut her short.

He shouts that everything he did was done
not as a free and privileged white man
biding his time on his father's plantation:
'Everything I did, with this head and these hands,
I did, not for a slave, Mrs Mason,
but for my Faith, for love, for my woman.'
Mrs Mason, dumbfounded, stares at Christy.
He loved and paid dearly. She's jealous and sorry.

After she sings Faith's praises as a slave
and woman who had grown to become a friend,
she turns her attention and his from Faith's grave
to the presumed dead, to me, the fruitful end
of his and Faith's ecstatic and brave –
even if short-lived and aggrieved – union.
She tells him everything she knows about me,
from my birth to my assumed death at sea.

She urges Christy to live his life his way
now that the two people he loves are lost.
She says he is her guest and should stay
as long as he cares. Since he is almost
family, she would love him to run the place.
He thanks her for being a consummate host,
but adds, 'I need proof of my son's fate,
just as this grave settles my wife, Faith's.'

Mrs Mason offers none, only hearsay
and conjecture and last sightings of me,
nothing concrete and therefore no mercy
for Christy from his quest, from what be-
comes in effect a new search and journey,
first Faith, now me, from mother to baby:
he must find the fruit of his love for Faith;
find me and prove love can trump hate.

Christy and Mrs Mason plant tulips
around Faith's grave: one for each hour
Christy and Faith lay in love's tight grip:
a puzzling, grand total of ninety-four.
He fills a pouch with topsoil from the pit,
kneels and lets Mrs Mason pray for
both of them, hugs and promises to come
with his son before those tulips blossom.

She watches him walk away as one might
a life one never expects to encounter
again. She felt this when her 'guiding light'
left, though she begged him to reconsider.
The same numbness inside, the same tight-
ness across her chest, dry mouth and drier
eyes. You stay with her if you're in your grave;
above ground, you've no option but to leave.

She sees tulips bud and bloom and die,
ows more, but those bloom too, then more.
Season after season becomes one sigh
and longing look down the empty road for
signs of him until her river of tears dries
up, her skin cracks, misery blocks her pores.
Mrs Mason leaves orders and takes to her bed.
Her staff plant tulips; soon she is dead.

I see my parents together for so long
they outlast Tom and Stella. An old Faith
and slightly older Christy, never a furlong
between them, in a fenced pasture, adrift
on a sea of peach grass, on furlough
from history, free of the harness of that fifth
column, skin, having shed theirs eons ago
for heart, life's only worthwhile cargo.

He has lost his hair and drive, she has lost
her good looks, but theirs is still a sweaty
love-nest where the worn body cannot exhaust
kisses and cuddles, back-rubs and belly
tickles, and for each to say, 'I love you' costs
as little as parted lips, lifted tongue and a breath:
when the next breath runs out, love runs out too;
therefore every breath should say, I love you.

Christy and Faith's love survives their deaths.
They go hand-in-hand into the black and blue.
It's lights-out for the shells that housed their breaths,
and eternity for the love shared by those two:
the black, starred night and the blue tent pitched
by infinity from this moment into the fu-
ture of what we can't know, unless we grapple
with our past and this earth before people

sprouted on its face and spread all over,
building anthills and burrows, turning forests
into savannahs, and aviaries into beds of feathers.
I realise men must build a place for work and rest,
but not this use-up and throw-away culture,
this promotion of our species and fuck the rest.
But I digress, I meant to say, when politics took over,
that I wish we had treated the world like a lover:

to obey, worship, serve at love's altar;
to move through and learn from it; hang
onto nature's web and spin like a spider;
to see that web in the morning light strung
with dew; to smash our faces at the glass of a
well or stream; not wake and cry like Caliban
for the same dream of what could have been
on this earth had we looked at it and really seen.

I and I

Right now, rain so hard it stings. I wash
in its shattered glass until I am raw,
tender, inside-out. I can't be caressed.
All my days are like this: too much wa-
ter and light – their ice-picks on my iris –
to stray outside. The sky has one flaw:
emptying itself of light and water;
unburdening itself on my shoulders.

Earth, be my mother. Hug me for free.
Sky, father me. Lift me. Throw me high,
catch me and set me down gingerly as a bee
on a flower in my mother's water and light.
I bathe in light. I wear a coat of sleet
sewn with thread borrowed from the sky.
The Mighty Sparrow sings me to sleep.
My round mother bears me on her back.

I have no one left on earth to speak of.
No flesh and scent I can follow away
from harm. No names to drop, or trip off
my tongue. No 'mother' or 'father' to say
without thinking. Only a gap big enough
for me to spend the rest of my days
between earth and sky, my cloudy head
humming full of Slavery's towering dead.

The ground draws me under year by year.
The sky digs and pulls weeds from my scalp.
My stretched bones in between, my slack, bare
body of skin's faded and sodden burlap
hardly contains my sticks and stones and fears.
Lanceolate light stabs the back of my eyes, slaps
paint behind the lids, disconnects the wires
in my head, fuses one vertebra to another.

My joints solidify. I heave and wade
through calcified light, my body no longer
mine and portioned out between the dead.
Dear God, let me be anything but younger.
I steady my pupils to admit more lead
for light, bare my pale tendons for water
to sever, invite the sky to peel off my skull,
gorge the delicacy inside until quite full.

Without a mother and father I am nothing.
Water and light, earth and sky, divide me.
Take me out of history, make a neutral being
of me; the colour of light, let me be
subtle as water, pliable as I imagine
the sky to be: open, contained, stretchy,
impenetrable and osmotic like skin;
able to keep things out and hold things in.

He never finds me, that man calling himself
my father. He criss-crosses time zones
in search of me, falls asleep in a makeshift
shelter and never wakes; dying alone,
he is buried at the roadside by drift-
ers in an unmarked grave and his belong-
ings divided among them as their fee
for a job well done – they have set him free:

a cross, tied with leguminous wisteria,
plunged at his head, a stone to beat it down.
Instead, *I* find *him* in the immaterial
pub talk of his grave-diggers and my own
ears tuned for another episode in my serial
misery, my quarrel with history, my brown
skin and blues against history's black
and white, my rainbow coalition attack.

It costs a few rounds of drinks to obtain
directions to the tree dividing the road.
They say to look beside a ditch or drain,
gully or trench. The grave is new and broad
to accommodate a boxer's unruly frame.
Turned earth shines its death-shroud,
not earth so much as death, deaf to all pleas
for clemency from suffering, to die with ease.

Little swelling marking the ground of a man
cut down early, with soil for linen and no name,
answer me! Was he suffering from the chills and,
with his feet pointing the way he came,
mistook soil for linen and a stone made of sand
for a pillow? Does his head point towards home,
his final destination, the place of his dreams,
a journey to be continued by other means?

Not by boat, nor cart, nor mule nor horse,
not even on foot, but as pollen, dependent
on seasons and the generosity of others.
I take him with me, a little memento –
bedding from his earthly bed that gathers
in wind and rain, and is rooted, until redundant
as a covering, by wild boar, taper, vole
and the anvil-headed, myopic mole.

I pull the weeds, straighten the cross, pray
for his sake, and continue in my carriage
up the road, following his lead that some day
there must be a place where the marriage
of men and women regardless of race stays
sacrosanct, impervious to the sacrilege
of hate, sanctioned by the muse of love,
present in the ground below and the air above.

I end up at Mrs Mason's, with a deed
in my name, and in a jam that's extant:
no one left to love me, all dead who did.
I care for the earth as one would a parent
in her dotage. I let it run to pasture, weed
and shrub, hand out parcels to servants.
Every day I paint the sky a colour
unlike any sky witnessed before.

I never convinced anyone to learn
anything by my example other than keep
breathing, draw hard on air, the burn
of life, put one foot forward to meet
something always ahead worth earn-
ing as you chop your way clear to greet
someone unexpected also clearing a course,
who greets you in similar surprise.

condemned

..s all the conditions

..o being somehow mend:

..and all its ramifications

..nfazed into the new millennium.

..ing that I see in countries and nations

..s me this is true: Slavery may be buried,

but it's not dead, its offspring, Racism, still breeds.

What have I inherited? I am standing
on the spot wanting direction. My head
flits about without understanding
anything. It empties and instead
of reaching a point of peace, ascending
the ladder brings more rungs to ascend.
Slavery cultivates worries, plants distress;
history sows little, reaps even less.

I am the lives of slaves. Every move
I make obeys orders from an overseer.
First he is a whip, a kick, a rude
mouth, a fist and spit, yes sir, no sir,
before he is a man, only to drive
his manhood into a slave woman. Her
days are his and nights she hides from him.
He is white and black, stranger and kin.

His voice reverberates inside my skull.
His big hands transport me off my feet
by clamping the sides of my head. I am his kill
if he wants me. I hang. His stare defeats
my flesh, crumbling my bones, withering my will.
When he drops me, I walk the sides of neat
squares. In a quadrille for slaves and slavers,
I am partnered by Time. Time is my master.

Time, please grant me immunity
from the overseer. I dream I am
headless. His lips move with impunity
but I can't read them. His crushing hands
descend and there is only the purity
of air to meet their grip. His whip lands
on my back and all the whips of Slavery
cast lightning and thunder on my bravery.

I see his feet as two trunks on an estate
of trees. My mind frames an axe, I grip
an axe handle. I swing at those two stakes.
I don't stop swinging until I have ripped
the pylons from their moorings. I take
time to reduce the trunks to logs stripped
of their bark, bark stripped of its bite;
I make a bonfire that burns bright.

Surrounded by my inheritance, immersed,
daily telling myself I am a dog-eared mule
to be laden, beaten, ridden, harnessed,
my immortal side bends all the rules
that keep my slave side well versed
in hard work, hoping to kill the soul
by wrecking the body. I am master,
slave and overseer bringing disaster.

I criss-cross four time zones looking
for faults to do with race and find plenty
to write home about. I try unhooking
myself from the obligation to empty
the States of hate so I can make a booking
with my flight from immortality.
Then I bump into a child who's raped,
a man who's beaten and I can't escape.

I try staring at the sun to cauterise
my mind. A sun too big for its frying pan.
A worry far bigger than my body. I realise
that I cannot kill what I don't understand
and, even if conscience were dead, my eyes
would still see what even the blind can:
that you can't side-step or throw out history;
and the past is present in future stories.

My head pounds. I break its names, shelved
neat as china in a cabinet given pride of place
in a room reserved for visitors only, an unlived-
in room, one that stores air, light and malice
for generations to dust, polish and delve
into for more resentment to crease the face:
names I should remember and don't, dates
that tell me when I had first cause to hate.

I erase the features of faces that bear
striking resemblance to mine, but the more
I rub out, the more admonishing their stares
become. My strokes, meant to polish the floor,
scratch it instead. I stoke the very fire
I set out to smother. I open the door
to that ancestral cabinet and crush
every piece of china inside into dust.

The lives seem small now, the dilemmas
smaller. My need to correct some wrong
done to me and people like me smaller
still. I hide from those who rehearse songs
of sorrow for a better tomorrow. I holler
at them to take their anthems of woebegone
elsewhere. I am the singer and the song –
lest you forget – wrong-doer and wronged.

Ancestors hunt at night so I lie low and spout
poetry from memory – the best suitcase
I ever packed. I hear them knock out
a man's brains using the very rock he placed
in his jacket and rested his head on – how
he snored through it all; how his face
shone and the peace that settled on
it hardly fluttered in all the commotion.

I hear so much I do not care for.
I live beside a stream whose whispery
twists and turns, ups and downs, murmur
about a life much like my own misery.
My past bubbles barely below the sur-
face; sometimes the current's trickery
backfires and all I detect is applause:
water bending backwards to appease

rock, gravity, air, rhythm and light.
Five masters to serve and five reasons
water cannot win this ceaseless fight.
Learn to fold under pressure like the seasons.
Be blind in your progress, let touch be your sight.
Dodge water's caress – it erases stones.
Water gives shape to light; gravity's a stair.
Water climbs up and down ladders of air.

I want to die. The past won't let me leave.
While other people expire, pressed
into the service of the past, I breathe.
My brains soak in Slavery and, for the rest
of time, that past promises to preserve
me as long as slave conditions persist.
The statutes written in the blood of martyrs say no;
Dickson Road in Eltham, London, says so.

Stay away from water. Do not listen
however closely it approximates
to your name. Forget you were christened.
When you hear an announcement on a P.A. wait
for what comes next, a no-sound likened
to a one-hand clap, or commensurate
with stepping into the same stream twice,
impossible unless that river were ice.

Strangers are polite with flesh that belongs
to them. They handle me as they'd wish
to be handled, buried standing in an oblong
box carved from eucalyptus whose lavish
smell keeps them company as the worms
have their way with them; keeps them fresh.
I figure out all this while I am washing
crouched under a stand-pipe gushing

my name among other impurities.
I breathe water. I do not choke or burn.
A crowd gathers and one of them empties
paraffin on me. Either I am too stubborn
to catch alight or the famous humidity
softens their matches. I start to run,
they give chase. My crime? I only
failed to read the sign, Whites Only.

I swear there was no sign, just a belief
governing the use of that public pipe.
I run into the strong arms of the police
who charge me – after a mild whipping
for not knowing better – with disturbing the peace.
I pace my cell all through the night,
crushing the winged shells of cockroaches,
nursing my two-hundred-year-old headache.

Live and let live, I hear you say. Sure,
when I can move freely from A to B,
or speak and write freely and not incur
the wrath of a race who wishes to keep me
in my designated place. I'll side-step lower
life-forms than me. I will gladly be
a Jain and carry a broom everywhere
sweeping the path absolutely clear.

The cops escort me from their jurisdiction.
I wander into the next town and find a bar
named, Forget Me Not. The compunction
for my race has seen every avatar:
I don't pick fights, rows choose me, ructions
like my company; no matter how far
I go to avoid them, they always try
harder, reading 'Welcome' for my 'No Entry'.

The rum and Coke have not passed my lips
when a man snuffs his cigarette in my drink.
I lift my head to see his face and he slips
a knife from his trouser pocket and sinks
it into my chest. It burns with the same grip
as that squandered rum my instinct
told me to miss but my throat cried out for;
pain radiates outwards throwing me to the floor.

If he's any good he should follow through.
He stands over my body as if that
is exactly what he intends to do.
Instead, he steps over me lying flat
and he exits into the zinc-hot afternoon.
Eyes chase him out the door then swivel back
and settle on me. The ambulance arrives.
They tell me he just missed my arteries.

They make small talk as they bandage
my chest ignoring my grimace. I bolt down
a fresh rum on the house offered after the manage-
ment extracts my promise to leave town.
I insist on paying and don't take the change.
For once there's a throb in my chest sown
by a hate that is stronger than my heart;
it weeps, it feeds, it beats, it scares, it hurts.

I find the railway line and hop on a train,
heading on logarithmic lines through valleys
with slabs of steel for company and a pain
in my chest, snatching sleep despite the artillery
testing of wheels on the tracks and the engine
chewing up the quiet country and capillaries
of light shooting through the rapids of gaps
in the carriage to fall on me in stars and stripes.

I hope with time to close the second mouth
opened at chest level, to stop it dribbling
my private business in such an uncouth
manner leaving my first mouth incredibly
high and dry. If not a mouth, a cyclops'
oracular eye. If not an eye, a cradle
bearing the child who carries the seeds
of my destruction: I die as I bleed.

Yes, dying. That blade was extraordinary:
wielded by God, Devil, or Fate, or an agent
acting on their behalf, it missed my artery
by miles in biological terms; the real target
being my soul. I ask myself if I am ready
to die and leave Slavery and feel no regret
that white remains white and black is black
and the two, belly to belly, back to back.

I chase the answer to that conundrum!
I fight off Death. Outrage keeps me alive.
Neither black nor white, I am rubicund,
poised between the two, not on either side.
For two centuries I've been trying to abscond
from the responsibility of righting the slide
of both races into deeper cycles of hell;
Up From Slavery, Booker T's hardsell.

This train I'm on's really bound for glory.
This train – going by the light seeping in –
is nothing if not extremely holey.
Hallelujah! This is not a gravy train.
That's something poetry can never be.
Though it can bring with it a little fame.
My train is death but the engine is my craft.
Death wins but poetry gets the last laugh.

I make it to the other side of the century.
Somehow black people free themselves.
All the bones above ground begin to bury
in wind and rain. The bright bones of slaves.
Their porous, shapely, desecrated bodies.
Those who were used as muscles all their lives.
The old in black on walks at noon, with large
umbrellas stroll to their deaths slow as a barge.

The young walk as if stepping on sponge,
gesture so big the cobweb they seem to clear
before them must cover an entire lounge.
Their speech is loud, explosive, nuclear.
Laughter from them echoes on the flagstone.
When they cry the house drains clutter.
They are not flesh and bone but titanium,
melting only when they hear the word mom.

This train I am dying on pulls into a station
without a platform. The carriage loses its sides.
A crowd greets me with a standing ovation,
transporting me by hands over their heads
towards a bright figure I have no notion
about other than to say it feels warm and alive.
My particular life pales next to this source;
I stop being me when I fall into its embrace.

I, or the me that once was, don't expect
to see company but I, the me that is
unrecognisable to myself, see perfected
(bathed in the same giddy radiance as
the day they eloped) Faith and Christy, and next
Mr and Mrs Mason, younger than I visualised,
and Tom and Stella. We run to each other.
They hug the new me, knowing me better

than I know myself. And for the longest while
we are one flesh and bone and blood,
at the same time as our timeless ethereal
selves, so that everything I want to know floods
my new condition in a flash. We are all smiles –
or more accurately, since we are bod-
iless, a condition of smiling prevails;
gravityless, the light fills us and we sail.